Joseph M. Monks

STUFF OUT'A MY HEAD

*illustrations by
Bernie Wrightson*

CHANTING MONKS PRESS

The characters and events in this book are fictitious. Any similarity to real persons, living or dead, is coincidental and not intended by the author.

Stuff Out'a My Head
by Joseph M. Monks

Paperback Edition ISBN 0-9726604-0-2
Hardcover Bound In Black Edition ISBN 0-9726604-1-0

Chanting Monks Press
www.chantingmonks.com

Stuff Out'a My Head © 2002 Joseph M. Monks
All rights reserved.

All stories © 2002 Joseph M. Monks
All interior artwork © Bernie Wrightson
Cover design by Hart D. Fisher

Printed in the United States of America
First Printing: November 2002

Chance Meeting
page 5

Tokens
page 13

Brutal
page 27

Coven
page 40

The Monthly
page 49

p0rn
page 89

*For my friends and family,
most of whom are wondering,
"What the hell did* we *do wrong?"*

CHANCE MEETING

B L L   L

The familiar *ting!*

As the doors whoosh open an awareness of the canvas rope straining on the soft flesh of the left wrist becomes evident. Again. The newspaper can offer only a minor diversion.

Especially with its ugly headline.

Funny, comes the thought, *it's a little too late for a repairman.*

The weight is shifted from left foot to right, heel to toe to avoid the little pins and needles of fatigue. The laundry bag's weight shifts, too, almost leaning forward enough to spill free the plastic detergent bottle. A jerk of the irritated wrist moves the cord, free to pester fresh skin, but the bag returns to its upright position.

13

The doors close with no other entrants and a silent sigh escapes. Ten hours behind the counter and two hours of laundry has created a thankfulness for lack of company and the fewest possible stops.

Not much of a smell for a gear jockey.

Especially this late.

Funny, comes the thought, it *is* late for a repairman.

4   5   6   *ting!*

The doors open, stick a little in the middle, spit out a noise of effort, and split apart.

The hallway is empty. Each party gives a little lean towards the middle, a brief glance, and a shrug. A look is exchanged, the first, and the repairman stabs at the number **13** for a second time. **18** still remains lit and still seems an eon, and a mile away.

Pretty clean uniform, too.

The hat reads "New York Boiler Co." embroidered on a crisp brown corduroy cap. The uniform is brown, too, with a few odd stains too tough for Tide to have removed.

Must be new, even the work boots look clean. So does the work belt. There are smudges of oil and mystery sludge on the pale leather, but no frays or torn loops. The hammer, wrenches, wire cutters, screwdrivers, all seemed to be neat and in order.

Maybe he's new...

7   **8**

More noises. Louder this time, and most definitely mechanical. There's an echo from somewhere above, a clattering of chains and pulley-like devices. It's as if Jacob Marley was taking a walk down the very shaft itself.

9   **10**   **11**   **12**   *tiing!*

Another sigh escapes, this one not so silent, not so hidden. A glance from the repairman and a smile. A knowing smile. It's late, especially for a repairman, and so the smile must be knowing. After ten hours behind the counter and two hours in the ramshackle laundry room, with no air conditioning and the stale smell of hot dryer air permeating virtually everything, the shared knowledge, "overtime's a bitch" is understood even though unspoken.

The absence of fresh air is, within an instant, unsettling. The repairman is shifting his weight now, heel to toe, toe to heel with a certain minor impatience.

The doors have not opened.

No way, the thought comes, the laundry bag and the rope pulling at the flesh are forgotten, as are the pins and needles travelling up through the soles of her feet, *no way, not tonight...*

The repairman jabs at the lit **13** button several times, normally an annoying and useless action. Tonight it is welcome.

Very clean hands and fingers.

Especially for a repairman.

12   **13**

Grinding. A slow discontinuation of motion. Neither button is lit, and again, the doors do not part.

Oh shit...

Pressing the buttons proves futile, and the repairman cedes that loss after a few moments. He turns and sighs, facing his companion, both leaning against opposite walls of the car.

Exasperation is evident. The cord around the wrist is shrugged free. Somewhere, far below, there is a dull buzzing that each can only assume is the alarm, one of the buttons pressed with furtive urging moments earlier.

Yet another sigh. Pupils are focussed skywards although the lids are shut tight.

The thought comes: *Hey, a repairman.*

"Wish I knew something about these things," he states, his words remarked as casually as if he had read her mind. But he hasn't, he couldn't have. He's only staring at the panel where the emergency phone has been torn out, looking at what's been left behind: a meaningless jumble of multi-colored wiring and electrical tape, remnants from decades of past repair. And then he looks back.

"I see he did it again."

"Pardon?"

"Your newspaper, I was noticing that he, uh, he'd done it again."

There's really no need to glance at the front page of the tabloid. She has looked it over already. Dozens of times. But reflex requires it. The headline is bold and black, and the photo, of a sheet—stained dark over several areas that covered the curves and contours of a body, stared right back. The ugly topic of conversation, so prevalent at the service desk today, is now again thrust into her face.

"Oh, yeah," feeble and soft, trying to sound disinterested.

"Wonder what it's going to take to catch him?"

"I'm sure the police are doing their best."

"Yeah, but he seems to be pretty good at it."

"Good at it? That sounds so, so unusual."

There was a soft laugh, a chuckle. "Yeah," the repairman responds upon a quick reflection, "guess you're dead right about that."

Was the pun intentional? The question didn't need to be asked. For the second time, eye contact, then brief silence.

"What do you think?"

"Think?"

"About catching him. Think they will?" The question seemed more like a challenge, as if there was some bizarre form of camaraderie that existed between this blue-collar Joe and the creature who had been terrorizing the city for so many weeks. The repairman seemed able to identify with the hunted. It reminded her of a motion picture, where the killer was somehow made to seem...

Sympathetic?

"I think it will be very difficult for them."

"So, you think he's pretty good at it, too?" The look is not a look, or a glance, or eye contact any longer. It is the cold pride of a leer, as the repairman stares.

Is there actually pride behind those eyes? Was there somehow something to be proud about? In having murdered nine women and not yet having been caught?

Was there some mantle upheld in dismembering bodies and using foreign devices to sexually violate the corpses?

It was far too late, came the thought, *for this repairman to be out on a boiler repair call.*

"Pretty horrible stuff he does," came the boiler repairman's next offering. Perhaps, just perhaps he was playing the game, striking out some grisly conversation to manipulate her into a "can I buy you a drink, I sure need one" scenario.

"So I've read."

"Yeah? Well, I got a friend on the force, says that what the papers get isn't the half of it," he continued.

"Oh, really." The tone was definite: utter distaste. There was no element of curiosity displayed, only quiet disdain. There was no need to know more. He was not dissuaded.

"He's not, you know," the repairman offers.

"Not? Not what?"

Her undesired companion glances at the newspaper headline. She reluctantly drops her eyes, preferring to keep them on him.

BUTCHER CLAIMS NINTH VICTIM

the headline reads. Below it, the lead story's subhead:

Serial Surgeon Slices,
Dissects SoHo Art Dealer

"What they say, in the papers. Surgeon, butcher...all that stuff is bullshit—pardon my French. Sex maniac...none of that's right. That's misinformation the cops are feeding the press to make this guy think they don't know what's going on, but trust me, they do."

"It sure seems like you know a lot about this," she says, wary...guarded. She wonders if he's telling the truth.

"Yeah, says this guy really isn't playing the sex angle at all, it's strictly about the killing. This guy's a regular *Friday the 13th* character. I know it's really sick, but my buddy told me this guy took off the last girl's nipples with a wire cutter. He's not this accomplished butcher with a cleaver or some med school reject killing women 'cause he can't get a date or flunked out of school. He's some freak. Doesn't really know anything about cutting, does a real hackjob. My buddy wasn't in on the first few, but he doesn't think the guy would even use a scalpel or razor. 'Too neat,' one of the forensic guys told him. Said this guy isn't about neat." The repairman looks away, down at the floor, shakes his head. "It's crazy! This whole world's going right down the toilet."

There was no immediate recognition of anything out of the ordinary.

But why would a boiler mechanic be carrying electrician's tools on his work belt?

What was he doing with his own pair of wire cutters?

Swallow and a breath. The thing to remember is that there's no need to think anything is out of the ordinary.

Late for a repairman.
Even though the conversation is very, very one sided.
A very clean repairman.
At any moment, the doors will be opening, she reassures herself.
Was the alarm buzzer still sounding?
It didn't seem to be. Questions were jumping up left and right—Had he really pressed it, or was that something that had only been imagined? Or had he made it *look* as if the button had been pressed, when it really hadn't been?
"Could you?" he asks.
"Could *I*?"
"Do you think *you* could?"
"Could *what*?"
"Kill? That way? Do you think you could do something like that?"
The fingers of the repairman's right hand are rubbing together, thumb to fore and middle finger. He's anxious, awaiting the response. He's brought it this far, the response must be correct.
Very, very late for a repairman...
"I guess if I had to, I could."
The eye contact remains cold. The car jerks for a second, and then there is silence, leaving the uneasy quiet between the two. Somewhere, far below, there's another grinding noise, and the whirr of machinery.
12   **13**
Both light up.
"If I met this killer, if I had to, I do believe I could."
The repairman lurches and corrects his balance momentarily as the car jerks to life and motion is regained. The cord of the laundry bag is swiftly back around her wrist and the newspaper is folded in half.
13   *tiing!*
"Here." The newspaper is offered and for the last time their eyes meet.
"Oh, thanks."
"Well, you are working late."
And on the 13th floor.
"Oh, I'm not working here, I live here, just moved in."
"Oh, well, nice meeting you."
"Uh, yeah, see ya'," he finishes before the doors close.
14   **15**   **16**   **17**
The sigh is loud and long. The cord at the top of the laundry bag is pulled taut and digs into the raw flesh of her wrist. She ignores it. A noticeable shudder courses through her.
18   *tiing!*
The hallway is empty, but there's still an extra glance each way to confirm the absence of others. Once behind the door to her unit, it is locked by the double

dead bolt and by key, before the lights are even turned on. The laundry bag lands on the couch-bed with a thud, spilling most of its contents into the balled up plastic sheeting. It rests beside copies of all the metropolitan dailies save the one sacrificed to the "repairman."

Too late for a boiler repairman.

On the 13th floor.

The floor used for tenant storage, since there are no apartments on it.

It had been soooo close, this time.

The edges of the razor sharp scissors clip and trim each and every article, each and every mention of the media-dubbed "New York Butcher." Cut to size, they easily found space in the hardback photo album that served as a scrapbook.

"Too late for a repairman, but not a maid," she sounded, sorting a plastic case from the other contents of the laundry bag.

The nipples had dried swiftly and intact, and remained hard and erect in the see-through baggie. These would not flatten when pressed into the scrapbook, she decided, and grinned with the success.

The wire cutters went back into a box which she concealed in a hiding spot beneath the sink. She folded her legs beneath herself in an easy chair and took up the remote, quickly turned on the television.

Eleven o'clock.

Just in time for the network news. She always tried to make it home in time for the headlines.

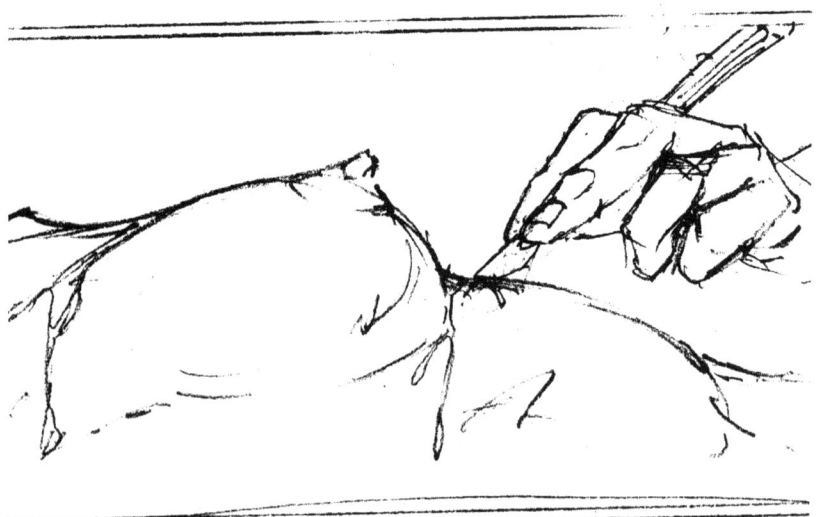

TOKENS

Wallace stared dully out the double glass doors of the Princess Emporium, peering through the grimy, smudged ghosts that no amount of neon and flashing lights could make disappear. He sat, eyes focusing on a tarnished coin sitting as yet unnoticed by the shuffling pedestrian traffic coming down 42nd Street. The sun had disappeared from the sky—at least for this part of the city—and now the street was lit with halogen. Nightfall was creeping across Manhattan. As the daytimers were leaving, the night owls were just beginning to rise.

Soon baby—Wallace reassured himself, *ain't gonna be much longer now. . .* He put a broad hand to his face, dug his thumb and index fingers into his temples, and rubbed in rough circles. Trying to ease the pounding, trying to rub the tension out of his brain. Rubbing harder. Unsuccessful.

Somewhere in the distance he heard it, a low grumbling turning into an angry roar. An animal sound, a demonlike roar. It grew in his head, the sound swelling in each ear, a two-pronged assault on his auditory sense. It sounded long and harsh, gradually dying out hollow and empty, the echoes rang in his head, setting his teeth on edge before dropping from his ears into the pit of his stomach. . . . Only his imagination, he told himself, only his imagination. But somewhere, he knew the roar *was* sounding...somewhere indeed, the demons were howling for more...

Yearning...

Hungry...

Soon, Wallace hoped, soon—*before it grew unbearable, before it had gone too long, before...*

Then he saw it happen, a glint of light flashing off the crest of the coin—light from nowhere in particular. A single ray, source unknown. Perhaps reflected off the fender of a passing car, or the side of a shiny aluminum attaché case swinging in the tired hand of a businessman who had worked way too late, underappreciated by bosses working summer hours, his uncompensated overtime going again unnoticed. Maybe it had ricocheted like a stray bullet, initial path gone terribly awry after hitting a piece of gaudy costume jewelry. Maybe it had springboarded off a badge...whatever, wherever, it didn't matter.

Suddenly, the coin was glittering, shining like gold.

It had been seen.

The boy who had been the first to take notice of the coin bent and picked it up hesitantly, people brushing up against him as they bustled by, moving around him as if he were a signpost, or a mailbox, or the typical gift of some city dog—an obstacle to skirt on their way to various points of nowhere in particular. He stood up and stared at the coin in hand, then turned his head, looking at the double doors of the Emporium. His free hand moved to his back pocket, bringing out his wallet. In it, the freshly laminated ID card he'd placed there earlier in the afternoon. The card identified him as being eighteen, but his face betrayed that fantasy and the truth of every one of his fifteen years.

Watching the boy's action out of the corner of his eye, Wallace felt his heart jump as his chest tightened involuntarily—nobody had ever passed up the coin before, but, just the same, nobody had ever taken this long to come on into the shop, to take advantage of the freebie. Wallace felt a knot growing in his stomach—he was a boy, after all—and there was a moment where he realized that the rumbling going through his gut was perhaps rebellion at the impending corruption of the youth. Wallace swallowed hard, the saliva suddenly gone from his mouth - *It was still his choice, after all*, Wallace thought, justifying the situation to himself—*the boy still had to be the one to make the choice...* Wallace swallowed hard again. The boy was coming in.

In the moment it took for the boy to walk through the double glass doors, Wallace sized him up—he was a first timer, no doubt. Wallace placed mental odds at five-to-one that the kid wasn't even from the city, *probably an Island boy, a soft kid from the suburbs. Or maybe down from one of the expensive Westchester County hamlets to the north. Total rookie...totally clueless.*

The boy had a soft face, noted Wallace. Round cheeks still with a hint of teen baby fat in them, bright eyes, a neat haircut cropping his dirty blonde hair to the base of his neck, clad in the typical uniform of the average American high schooler—blue jeans, too-expensive high top basketball sneakers that had never been worn on a court, a white T-shirt emblazoned with the logo of some band Wallace never heard of, and a denim jacket.

It was always easy to spot the first timers, and this kid proved to be no exception. Every sight in the Emporium was new to him, everything he viewed a curiosity. Wallace watched as the boy drank them all in fascination. Evelyn was leaning over to allow a fifty-five year old regular a better view of her ample bosom, her provocative stance practically allowing her sagging tits to spill out of her yellow, tattered bra. Over by the window, Nina was wiggling her own wares, playing fancifully with the stand-up neon erection beside the magazine rack. The expression on the boy's face—a mix of innocence and wide-eyed amazement—said it all. Evelyn let Roger, the regular, grope a handful of knocker before playfully slapping his hand away. Later, she would let Roger take her to one of the private booths, soak him for most of his SSI check before sending him on his way, his wallet empty and his shorts stained. Same old, same old.

As he wandered closer, walking past Maria holding her trademark banana, and Louie, another one of the regulars engrossed in the latest issue of *Tits & Clits*, Wallace, suppressing all of his earlier emotions and doubts, launched into his spiel.

"Hey, hey," he began, looking directly at the boy and making eye contact. "C'mon in, sir, and welcome to the Princess Emporium! Finest showplace in all of New York City! What might I be able to help you with my man, some fresh video? Books? Leather goods? Maybe a private meeting with one of our special ladies?" At this point, Wallace backed off a bit and waited—having gotten the boy's complete and total attention, he let the cool, thin smile stretch across his face.

"Uh, I dunno..." stammered the youth, taken aback and put a little off guard by Wallace's cheery confrontation. "Uh, nothing, really, I'm just, uh, looking around."

"Well, whatcha have in mind there, then, dude?" pestered Wallace, throwing a hint of agitation into his voice, clearly signalling to the kid that Wallace thought the boy was wasting his time. He let the tone of his voice dictate the situation. Made it sound like he was challenging the boy. Steering the cherry towards something more...aggressive.

"Uh, maybe..." the boy responded, still overwhelmed by his surroundings and trying to bluff his way through his inexperience. Just as he was beginning to panic, feeling that he was in way over his head, his attention and gaze was caught by Corrine, a busty, curvaceous Latin who paid the two of them no mind. She was wearing nothing but red high heels, pasties, and a string of anal floss that was pulled so deep into the crack of her ass that it was essentially invisible. She was heading down a flight of stairs just to the right of Wallace's podium which led deeper into the Emporium.

"Aah," said Wallace knowingly, "the man sees something he likes.' Now his voice was smooth, enticing, almost friendly. It was like Wallace was sharing something, like there was now some sort of understanding between them. "Maybe the man ought to go downstairs there and take him a look-see, maybe find something he really wants."

The boy turned his head back towards Wallace, still struggling to make up his young mind. Wallace had seen a million cherries before him, trying to make up their mind one way or the other. Which type would this one be? Gutless Mama's boy who'd pocket the coin as a souvenir, or the kind who would yield to his curiosity. Wallace could tell that the boy was just getting past the worried stage, growing emboldened by not having been thrown out of the Emporium, not having his phony ID checked, not having been caught. Now he just had to deal with the actual working of the place.

"Think I will," he finally replied, and this time when he spoke there was a hint of confidence behind the words. He was staring at the staircase leading down to the lower levels of the Emporium, moving towards it. Towards where he had seen Corrine disappear moments earlier.

"Hup, hup, now hold on just a sec," intervened Wallace, "you gonna need some tokens before you go takin' off down there. They're four for five dollars."

"Uh, that's okay," the boy stated, reaching into his pocket and fishing out the coin he'd picked up out on the sidewalk, "I've got one already."

Wallace looked at the coin in the boy's hand skeptically, his brow furrowed and his expression conveying to the youth a sense that he had just said something dizzyingly stupid.

"That's only good for the Lower Level, for all the booths, the machines, all the tokens are like this—didn't you get any of these last time?" Wallace asked.

"Oh, yeah, that's right," the boy weaseled, "I forgot." He removed a crumpled five dollar bill from his front pocket and placed it on the counter, scooping up the four small tokens in one hand as Wallace slipped the money into the cashbox. The boy turned and smiled, taking a deep breath as he moved towards the stairs, hoping that his gaffe hadn't targeted him as being what he was, an underage boy in a Manhattan porno shop, as out of place as condoms in the Pope's nightstand. Wallace noted the change in the boy's demeanor and smiled as the youth quickly hustled down the stairs, tracing Corrine's path. Now, Wallace knew, the tension of possibly getting caught was once again with him

The boy descended the stairs and disappeared from sight. Wallace nodded silently to himself while Maria rubbed the banana between her greasy breasts for Louie.

Everything was going as planned.

Once at the base of the first flight of stairs, the cherry was finding that things were more than twice as active as what he'd been witness to upstairs. Signs, some neon, some hand-painted, some scrawled in handwritten magic marker and taped over older ones, directed potential customers to a variety of different pleasures or perversions, depending on your point of view. There were large hanging placards for a string of video booths—each costing a single token for limited time viewing. Just beyond, a blinking, gaudy neon number showcased a row of stalls in which, for a mere two tokens, any patron could bear witness to LIVE SEX ACTS: SPECTACULAR! EXOTIC! UNNATURAL!

Unnatural?

Several phone-booth styled stalls had been designated the *Oral Palace*, where, for a single token, one could view a live woman practicing her talents on inanimate objects through a pane of glass. Pictures outside the booths showed women wrapping their lips around dildos, vibrators, even objects so large that they had to be representative of the animal kingdom. Some of the doors to the booths and stall were closed, concealing the inhabitants, while others, whether occupied or not, simply stood wide open. Passing one booth in particular, the youth felt his heart jump as he caught view of a man inside. The patron could have been no younger than sixty-five, holding a ratty looking yellowed phone receiver in one hand, masturbating furiously with the other. Behind the pane of glass a flabby, saggy black woman was licking a wet swirl around her nipple while a blinking red light indicated that it was time to insert another token. The old man groaned as he dropped the receiver into the crook of his neck and fished a token free from the pocket of his trousers, loose and open around his knees.

Walking quickly past, down the central hallway and beyond, deeper into the belly of the Princess Emporium, the kid slowed his gait, looked around, perused a magazine rack, trying not to appear too out of place. He canvassed the sampling of titles, many of which he could find at the 24-Hour Sippy Mart— *Hustler*, *Penthouse*, *Voluptuous*, *Naughty Neighbors* and some others—before going wide-eyed when he was confronted with what was pictured on the covers of such hard core favorites as *Greedy Cum-Gobblers*, *Black Leather Fetish*, and *Shaved 'N Smooth*. The tokens, rattling in his pocket, were also burning a hole in it. Looking around, he watched as the faces blended into the seedy surroundings. He was still being cautious, scanning the crowd for any sign of a familiar face, wondering whether it would be worse for him to be recognized here by anybody who might have known him—or to recognize someone he himself knew. Realistically, he estimated that there was only the slimmest of chances that either scenario would occur, especially considering he was a fifty-five minute train ride from home. Still, he viewed each passerby as a potential acquaintance of his father, the city-employed parent of a friend, or even a customer of his mother's decorating firm.

After slowly strolling the entire level, he found his way to a remote video booth that wasn't in use and got up the nerve to enter. Once inside, he closed the door immediately and surveyed his surroundings.

The booth was narrow and cramped, a small, wooden bench-seat built into one wall, with a low ceiling housing a single red bulb— the only source of light. The walls were painted a sickly shade of traffic cone orange, the bench a peeling, taxicab yellow. It wouldn't have surprised him at all if the paint had been stolen from a local auto body shop, leftovers from a job the city had probably overpaid for.

Before him, a grimy television screen was built into the wall above four arrow-directional buttons. Beside the screen was a single coin slot. Each of the arrow keys had a piece of tape below it, with either "Advance," "Review," "Slow Motion," or "Fast Fwd" as an option. The screen itself was displaying a poorly produced computer generated menu listing twelve different adult movies. All one had to do to watch any of them was drop a token in the slot and press the arrow keys until the desired film was highlighted. Inserting a token gave the viewer thirty seconds to alter his selection. Reading through the listing of films he found himself choosing between titles ranging from *Tight Anal Rampage 3* and *White Bun Busters* to *Black and Stacked* and *I Say Yes To Anything*...

Choosing one of the more generic titles, he dropped a single token into the slot and waited. There was a momentary hesitation, then a dull, mechanical whirring as the video player came to life. The computer lettering and the green background screen disappeared, replaced by a couple frolicking in a Jacuzzi, the camera poised at just the right angle to catch each and every penetration in dramatic close-up. After a few disinterested seconds he pressed the advance button, hopping to another film, this one offering a view of a girl who looked no older than he was. Her head was bobbing up and down in the lead male character's lap, his huge dick disappearing into her mouth as she sucked away on it noisily. This went on for almost a full forty-five seconds before a red light onscreen began blinking—the warning that the time on his token was about to expire. Without producing another token, the screen subsequently returned to the computer menu. The screen background had now turned into pale lavender.

A feeling of nervous apprehension gripped him as he opened the door to the stall, checking around to make sure that nobody was watching him in particular. Outside the booth it was business as usual, a few scantily clad women walking around, none of them particularly attractive. There was no sign of Corrine, the girl he'd seen when he'd first entered the Emporium, and he wondered where she might have been *working* at the moment. So far, he was thinking to himself while continuing around the downstairs concourse, the whole trip had been far from what he had expected. The image he had in his mind on the train ride in from Long Island had been very different, nothing like what he had been exposed to since entering the Emporium. He did have to admit it was certainly a far cry from anything he'd ever seen back in the neighborhood. Even on the 'net, it wasn't like this, wasn't as weird as seeing it in person, seeing old geezers jacking-off out in the open, or girls walking around almost totally naked. Girls who were willing to touch themselves and stick things up inside them behind a pane of glass while people paid to watch. It was hard to believe it was really like this, that people could actually do these things.

The LIVE SEX ACTS sign blinked invitingly above an unoccupied booth, and, with some reservations, he chose to enter. Dropping two of his remaining tokens into the coin slot, he took his seat on the bench (once he was sure it was clean), and waited to see what was next.

In this particular booth, there were three rows of glass eye slats with black bars in front of them. Once the tokens had activated the mechanism, the black screen behind the glass rose and one could view what waited behind through the appropriate eye slat for one's height.

With the black screen raised, he could see that the Live Sex Acts booths all formed a circular enclosure, in the center of which sat a bed occupied by a couple who were, at first, tough to see at all due to the lighting of the place. Momentarily, though, he could make out the form of a heavy set black woman, crouched on all fours, with a scrawny middle-aged white man standing behind her. The man was wearing a pair of leather pants, holding a riding crop in his hand, and had pierced ears, a ring in his nose, and piercings in both nipples. A tiny chain hung from one nipple ring to the other, crossing a faded tattoo of a Kabuki dancer that resided on his chest. Every so often he would place a hand on her breast, or reach in between her legs, and if she reacted in the slightest to the contact he'd bring down the riding crop harshly against her buttocks. Even though the light was dim at best, there were welts evident all across the woman's posterior. It went on for a good two minutes before the black bars once again reappeared, obscuring his view. By that time, however, the boy had already left, wandering further along down the hallway, now hoping to find one more thing—the exit.

Could the Emporium really be this big? For one reason or another, the Princess Emporium suddenly seemed devoid of any exit signs. There was the option to return from whence he came, and just walk out the front door, but there had to be another way. He had seen signs before, EXITsigns that had directed him away from the main entrance, away from the man who had sold him the tokens. A man he was not anxious to see again. All he had to do, then, was find one of those signs and follow some other path out of the place.

At the end of the hallway he came to a second stairway, and not much else. The stairway, leading down another level, was disquieting. He wondered if by going further down, he could possibly catch an exit right into the subway system that had initially carried him here. He knew that several larger stations had lower level entries to shops, even shops like this. How far could he have been from Times Square? Or was it Grand Central...?

Above this set of stairs, however, was a hand painted sign that read "Lower Level." It brought Wallace's words back to mind, a reminder that the token he found out on the street, the one that had convinced him that the Princess Emporium was the place he would go, was only good down here—the Lower Level. Pulling the two remaining tokens free from the lint in his otherwise empty pocket, he could see the difference. The four for five dollar token he had left over was eight sided and small, no bigger than a quarter. The one he'd found out on the sidewalk was heavier and nearly the size of a half-dollar, with elaborate images embossed on each side. On one, the profile of a female dancer was clear and well rendered, on the other was a profile of a couple engaged in a sexual position. After examining both sides carefully, and comparing the tokens, he decided to keep the cheap one as a souvenir of the trip, and use the other one. After all, he found it—it had been free. Besides, the small token would be plenty enough a prize when he returned home and showed the gang. Few of his upper-middle class suburban cohorts had ever ventured into the city, much less alone and at night. They spent their summer evenings trolling the malls and at the sprawling cineplexes. The tale of this trip, he was certain, would inevitably open up brand new possibilities for him and his buddies.

One step down, he was convinced he'd made the right decision.

There was a small EXIT sign located at the bottom.

Walking down the stairs he became aware of the conspicuous lack of people around him. The more pressing thought, however, was just what this token might entitle him to. As he made his way down the steps and into another short hallway, he passed posters for films like *Deep Throat*, *Behind the Green Door*, and *The Devil in Ms. Jones*. The posters were faded and old, their corners curled, peeling away from the dingy, powder blue walls. Yellowed patchworks of scotch tape endeavored to hold them in place. It wouldn't have been surprising to find that they had been hung on the walls back when the films had first been released. He stopped to look at the copyright date down in the corner of one of them. It had been printed more than a decade before he'd been born.

A creeping sense of worry began growing within him. The idea that this token might be redeemable in any way for some form of contact was a very real fear. In this place, contact with anything was to be avoided at all costs. Who knew what any of the girls who worked here had? Who knew what they had done before, or were doing even now? If this token was indeed good for some sort of sexual contact or act, he wanted no part of it. He was curious, true, but there was no way he was going to catch some venereal disease over it. How would he ever explain that to his parents? He was supposed to be in Flushing, seeing the Mets play, not in Manhattan at some seedy porno palace.

At the end of the hallway there was a short, sharp bend, and, surprisingly, it ended just beyond that. Facing him was a narrow, white door, barely wider than any of the upstairs booth doors. Stenciled on it in boldfaced block lettering were the words:

The Ultimate!
The End-All
In
Erotic Sensuality!
1 Token

The door was slightly ajar.

He stared down at the large token in his hand, warm against the flesh of his palm. He wasn't certain if he wanted to continue. Behind the door, he knew, lay something that was obviously a bit more expensive and intense than anything that could be had for a four for five dollar token. Whatever waited for him on the other side of the door was likely tenfold beyond anything he'd seen thus far.

His mind raced wildly, thoughts spinning in his head, dizzying and chaotic —the thought of contact, AIDS, another man behind the door, all had him on the verge of turning and heading back upstairs, running the gauntlet again no matter what the cost in embarrassment. Even getting thrown out didn't seem as bad as it had when he'd first ventured in. In fact, there was something that would almost seem comforting about being thrown out—especially now. Out, after all, was all he really wanted.

He looked at the token. Then the door.

Wait, it's not like you have to do anything, he told himself. *It's not like you paid for it* or *anything...you found it.* He rationalized. Besides, there had been an EXIT sign. Somewhere after this was the other exit. Whatever was on the other side of the door, all he would have to do was ignore it and leave. That was well worth the big token, no matter what it would have cost had he paid for it.

Hell with it.

He went in.

The stuffy and tight booth was, at best, poorly lit. Upon entering, he found himself almost completely shrouded in darkness, and it took a few seconds for his eyes to adjust. Growing accustomed to the dimness, he began to make out the shapes he expected to find—the familiars. Before him, a large, full-length pane of glass, tinted so dark that he could not see anything through it, even when he cupped his hands around his eyes and pressed his nose against it. To his right, a coin slot in the wall, sized just right for the token he held in his hand. Another hand-stencilled sign above the slot:

ONE TOKEN.

Beneath that: PLEASE WAIT.

Full glass, he noted. A sigh of relief escaped. *Maybe there wasn't anything that was so special about this thing after all.* He smiled as he gave the token one last glance and dropped it into the slot.

The black cleft swallowed up the offering. The light in the booth extinguished itself . No video machine whirr, just the coin-path's noisy clatter, although at the end there was never any coin-box to bottom out into. *Please wait...* Eventually, the sound just died. Faced with silence, he waited.

There was a long pause before anything happened, but eventually he heard a grinding, mechanical sound and the dim light returned and increased, revealing a large, round bed some ten feet or so beyond the glass. There was a massive shape in the center of the mattress. Different parts moving in different directions. With the low lighting, and from where he was standing, he was actually somewhat disappointed.

A threesome? he thought, watching...*so that's the **ultimate**??? The End-All?* It was affirmed mentally—he was definitely disappointed.

The mechanical grinding began anew, and the glass wall before him began to rise swiftly into the ceiling.

*Oh no...*came the thought. Every apprehension and fear he had swept aside upon viewing the entanglement of bodies moving on the bed returned with a vengeance. He was so taken aback by the wall in front of him disappearing that he didn't notice that directly behind him, in the space between himself and the door, a second panel was descending. A panel with no knob or handle.

Turning around, it was obvious that there was no going back—the ultimate end-all was a one way ride, it seemed, and it was looking more and more like he was going to have to get through the room to get to the exit. Even in the faint glow cast from the red ceiling lights, there was a visible outline of a door on the far end of the room. It was going to be embarrassing, but he knew he was going to have to make his way past the surging mass of arms and legs writhing on the bed to leave.

It was uncomfortably warm down here, as if the room were being heated, or the activities on the bed had overcome the feeble air conditioning. On top of that, however, was the smell.

The smell, was atrocious.

The stench that infiltrated his nostrils was not unlike the one he caught when he had entered the subway station at 42nd Street and Grand Central Station. Coming off the inbound train, the subway tunnel reeked of stale urine, body odor and fumes, of sweat and heat and garbage and decay. He had stepped up his pace drastically, his nose wrinkled up in protest. Now, here in the room he was experiencing the same sensations. The stale scent of sex and sweat and heat made the room unbearable—it took a half-groan, half-whine from the bed to pull his attention back to more immediate concerns.

The room was large enough that, following along the wall to his right, it seemed entirely possible that he might not even be noticed if he went right for the door. Two steps towards that goal, however, that became impossible.

Music began to play, loud, obnoxious, carnival music. More glaring than the volume was the inappropriate tune—it raised the expectation that at any moment a carousel would appear, either from behind another screen, or perhaps spring up right out of the floor. At this point, as things were growing increasingly surreal, anything seemed possible.

Two more steps towards the door, the room lights went on. The light filled the room, not with a full red glow, but with brilliant, bright-white light. The whole room was illuminated, and for the first time since he entered the Princess Emporium, there was nothing hidden or obscured by darkness or softened by shadows.

A heartbeat later, taking one look towards the bed, Billy Lowell went completely out of his mind.

The thing on the bed moved. Billy could see now that it wasn't a group of three intertwined humans on the bed, rolling under the sheets in the raw, but instead something completely and utterly beyond comprehension.

It wasn't human at all...

The creature on the bed was amorphous, with tendrils oozing out from its center—if you could call it that. Blackish-gray fluid dripped from its gaping maw, droplets splattering the floor noisily in accumulating puddles. For eyes, it seemed, there were two misaligned, sunken masses. If it weren't for dark pupils in the center of each mass, these "eyes" could have been confused for pockets of milky-white pus. A sound escaped from the slathering maw, again, the half-groan, half-whine Billy had heard before. A single tendril rose up, and the whole creature seemed to heave along with it—not making direct motions per se, but rather flowing fluidly along with the momentum. The creature's whole body was encased in a viscous, slimy coating, and each motion was accompanied by a wet, sloshing sound. It lurched once towards Billy, then again, dropping completely off the bed and hitting the floor. It made a noise, not unlike the sound of a fish flopping onto a damp boat deck. It moved slowly towards where Billy stood, staring, trembling with fear.

Billy spun around, looking to escape. Behind him, however, the glass panel barred him from any hope of exiting. His hands sought out a latch or handle, some means by which he might pry the glass back up. Nothing.

He was trapped where he stood, unless he could get around the creature, unless he could get to the door across the room...

Turning once again to face the creature, Billy saw that it had closed the distance between them considerably. Now he could hear it breathing. Now Billy could make out the raspy, gasping noises as the creature sucked in air. He had heard a sound like it once before, when he had been younger. His grandfather had sounded like that sometimes, Billy remembered, when the old man had been in the hospital. He had come down emphysema, and every breath near the end had sounded like the noises the creature was making now—the same desperate wheezing for breath, but without enough lung power to draw oxygen.

Billy feinted to the left, then darted back to the right, trying to fake the creature out. On any of his friends, in any schoolyard in the country, the move—football tucked neatly under one arm—would have shaken even the best of pursuers. But this was no schoolyard. And this was no football game.

The grotesque, deformed beast hissed, and that same gray black fluid that coated its gelatinous husk sprayed through the air, a fine mist striking Billy's skin. Billy threw his hands up, recoiling in disgust. The fluid had a bad smell, like the dumpster behind the school cafeteria. But it wasn't just the smell that got him.

It *burned...*

A tendril coiled in mid-air and sprung, lashing out and wrapping around Billy's ankle like a tourniquet. Billy heard himself scream, then felt it die in the back of his throat. Staring at his ankle he watched as his flesh melted beneath a black mass of molten denim. His nose, having grown accustomed to the bitter smell of this basement dungeon, now wrinkled up again at the pungent odor of his own burning skin. While Billy struggled, other tendrils tensed then sprang out at him, encircling his other leg, the foot of a Nike, the thick, muscled portion of his upper thigh. The monster was now dragging him across the floor. Billy's sneakers scraping against the concrete in a futile effort to gain release.

His body gradually succumbed, his lower extremities entirely enveloped within the grasp of the beast's poisonous, acid oozing tendrils. Billy reached back with one fist and made to strike the creature in defiance. One swift tendril caught the blow in midair, wrapping up Billy's whole fist and forearm. Both were gone in the blink of an eye, leaving Billy to pull back a quavering, bloody stump. Blood pulsed into the air from the jagged, torn veins of his forearm. A shard of white bone jutted beyond the pulpy mass of seared muscle and tendons, a wisp of smoke trailing up from boiling marrow. Billy's whole body began to convulse, jerking spastically as he fell to the floor. Vomit began gushing out over his lips as he tried to mutter a few familiar words.

Our Father, who art in Heaven...

Before he could complete the prayer, he was engulfed by countless tendrils. They swept over his body, melting and absorbing his ribs, his soupy intestines, and finally his face. The last part of Billy to be stilled was his eyes.

It was 11:40 when Wallace turned over his duties to Spence, who had arrived for work late, as usual. Tonight the extra ten minutes had worn Wallace thin, and as he walked briskly down the stairs to the Lower Level, the one part of the Emporium that was off limits to all who worked there, he found that overcoming his combined fear and revulsion was becoming increasingly difficult.

He hoped that tonight hadn't been a bad one. Wallace hated cleaning up after the bad ones. Walking through the back door, the scent alone told him all he needed to know.

It had...it had been a bad one...

The creature was off in one corner, resting against a filthy, blood-spattered wall, pleasing itself sexually. Strewn about the floor were several unidentifiable body parts, hunks and chunks of the boy's undigested anatomy. What might have been a strand of intestine, no longer than a yard or so, squelched noisily beneath Wallace's shoe.

"*Shit!*" Wallace yelped, jumping back a step. He reached for the light switch and flicked it on, bathing the room in full brightness. The creature rolled its milky whites sorrowfully, and slithered a few feet nearer the man.

On the floor, between the two, lay the token. The creature turned its white eyes towards it, and Wallace followed the stare.

"Goddamnit!" spat Wallace angrily, "You didn't even finish all the bones! You never should have let things go like this! Never! *Do you hear me?* You shoulda seen a doctor, goddamnit, you shoulda seen a doctor when you first caught it , when you still had a chance...I, I fuckin' *begged* you..." choked Wallace staring down at the creature.

Of course, there came no reply, only the wet sounds of the creature's labored breathing.

"Is there anything, *anything* left of you in there?"

There was a long pause before the creature stirred, one ropy tendril uncurling and sliding forward along the bloody floor. It raised up before Wallace and hovered for a second, then spasmed. Wallace hadn't notice that it had gathered up the token, but watched incredulously as the coin dropped at his feet.

"*More?* What the?! Mother of god, are you crazy? I can't...I can't keep cleaning this up... I can't keep getting rid of this mess! Look at this place! *There's too much of this one left!*" protested Wallace.

The tendril nudge the coin closer. It sat barely an inch from the tip of Wallace's shoe. Wallace stared in silence, dumbstruck, then knelt down and picked it up.

"Okay...one more, one more." Wallace agreed, staring the creature in the eyes. The beast quivered a bit, jerking from side to side and Wallace took it as a sign that it was pleased. Wallace killed the lights and locked the door, heading through the back entrance into the Lower Level hallway.

Back in the narrow corridor he reset the sliding glass panel, waited for a moment and unscrewed the single ceiling bulb overhead. He turned, bit his lip, and pulled the sticky token from his pocket.

It dropped into the slot with a momentary clatter, before all was silent.

The glass panel began sliding up into the ceiling, and Wallace felt himself beset by the foul odor of the basement for the first time.

"Last one, Dad," whispered Wallace hoarsely, his voice wavering as he spoke—

"*Mealtime.*"

BRUTAL

"You gon' do this thing, a-ight?"
"Yeah, yeah man, of course." Ray-Ray was sweating. Today was the day. No turning back. Twelve pairs of eyes—or maybe more, because there was no reason to believe there weren't others watching, hidden away somewhere—were staring at him.
"So you gon' be cool, right? In, out, be done, be back, a-ight?"
DJ Kix was there, sitting back in an old Barcolounger smoking a joint. He was wearing his jacket. Some of the others were, too. Not all of them, though. It didn't matter. They didn't have to. Once you had one, everybody knew. People who never saw you before knew.
They just did.
Malcolm was who he was looking at, though. Malcolm ran the gig, Malcolm was the man. Staring down at Ray-Ray through a pair of Oakleys so dark Ray-Ray'd swear they were solid black. He wondered if it were true, the rumor that Malcolm had lost an eye in a fight and hadda have a glass one put in his head so he'd look right. Everybody remembered when Malcolm had gone away on the B&E and come back with the eye-patch. Nobody asked any questions once Malcolm was back. Maybe he'd told somebody, maybe Kennedy, his younger brother, but just as easily maybe not. Maybe not nobody. But there was still the rumor, and when the eye-patch had disappeared, the pitch-black Oakleys had replaced it. Ray-Ray had never seen Malcolm without them. According to street legend, nobody had or ever would. Word was that Malcolm even fucked bitches

wearing the glasses, that he showered with 'em on, slept with 'em on. Killed with 'em on.

"A-iiiiiiight?" Kennedy's voice cut into Ray-Ray and brought him back to reality, to the moment. No turning back. This far, nobody got out. You didn't have a choice. In was in, out was dead, simple as that. Ray-Ray had gotten this far. Now it was time for the last step. He was sweating, he knew, he could feel it cold and damp on his back here in the basement of an abandoned old tenement building. Condemned. He wondered if that was some sort of sign. He could hear the edge in Kennedy's voice. If he fucked up, it would be Kennedy and one of the others, probably one of the ballers like Razz or maybe Baby-D who did him. Either way, there was no choice now, no turning back, no fucking up. He turned to look at Kennedy.

"I said a-ight, G, in, out, be done, be back, be black, it's all good." Razz laughed, so did a few of the others. Of course, they'd all been here before. They knew.

Kennedy didn't laugh. He stared back at Ray-Ray and his lips tightened. Ray-Ray stared, too, eye to eye with his former childhood best friend. Somewhere along the way they'd drifted apart. Kennedy had moved on. When Ray-Ray first started coming around, he thought maybe him and Kennedy could be friends again, but the longer he hung with the crew, the more he knew it was impossible. Whenever he looked at Kennedy, he saw his eyes. Cold, dead, eyes. Kennedy looked a lot like that Samuel L. Jackson, a bad-ass mutherfucka who could turn that look on you, that *you about to die, boy* look. The only problem was Kennedy had that look all the time. It was in his eyes, like it'd been burned there. There was no turning it off. Sometimes, Ray-Ray wondered

what have you seen, Kennedy?
what you seen that made your eyes that way?
but he never asked. Nobody did.
They just knew.

Ray-Ray dropped his smoke to the sidewalk and stabbed it out with the toe of his Adidas. Old pair, didn't matter shit what he did with 'em. Wouldn't be wearing them ever again after tonight, anyway, and he'd had his eyes on a stylin' pair of Nikes anyway. $135 on the tag, but tomorrow that wouldn't matter none to Ray-Ray. All that mattered was today, and takin' care of business.

Ray-Ray was about to light another smoke when the door to the club opened across the street. He jabbed the unlit cigarette into the corner of his mouth, sucking in a breath and holding his Zippo open in one hand. She'd be coming out about now, sweaty and singing the last few bars of whatever song had been playing inside the club. Ray-Ray couldn't hear the music from where he was standing, if it was still playing at all. This close to four, sometimes there was no music left to play. Closin' time. That's why he knew she'd be walking out about now, probably alone

he hoped
with her head down and a purposeful stride as she headed home. Ray-Ray took a breath, and waited. Two girls came out, didn't look his way, turned their heads and walked off in the opposite direction. He watched them disappear, snapping a flame out of the lighter with a calloused thumb. Sucking in a hot breath on the unfiltered cigarette, he waited. And watched.

She'd be out any minute. It had to be four o'clock, if not a few minutes after. She'd be alone
he hoped
because she always was.

After all, that's why he'd chosen her.

Like he willed her to appear, she did. She stepped tentatively out of the club, took a look in either direction.

alone
he knew she would be

She put her head down, consciously trying to avoid any potential eye-contact with anybody she might meet on the street. That didn't take the bop out of her step, and Ray-Ray was pretty sure through the cloud of smoke he'd exhaled that he could see her singing to herself. Maybe out loud, but more likely mouthing the words to some hot hip-hop song.

He dropped the half-done smoke, left it burning in the gutter, stepped off the curb and fell into step. He felt his own stride, heavy and tense. He wanted the bop Jada had, wanted that spring in his step, but instead the sweat was beginning to crawl down his back again. He wondered what she was singing, tried to slow down so he wouldn't catch up so fast. He had to remember, he was taller, walking faster with longer strides, and this wasn't where he wanted to catch up to her. That wouldn't work out, that would fuck it up, fuck him up. He blinked away a bead of sweat and wished he'd been able to finish his smoke.

"You take it easy, Double-R, an' you be pimpin' with the crew." Kennedy's words came back to Ray-Ray as he slowed his pace. Kennedy had pulled him aside just before Baby-D had driven him to the club, dropping him off in a flashy, white Mercedes 380-I. Gold hubcaps, mirrored ground effects and a pair of slammin profile Lorenzos rollin' the track. Ray-Ray knew the deal when he stepped into the car. Givin' him a taste, gettin' his head ready for business. Kennedy's eyes burning into him as he whispered
encouragement?
his message. DMX was playing loud in the background, Kix had the volume crankin'.

Ya'll gonna make me lose my mind, up in here, up in here
Y'all gonna make me go all out, up in here, up in here
"You go all out, y'hear?"

Ray-Ray gave a nod as the Mercedes door opened and he swung inside. He didn't say anything back to Kennedy as the tinted windows rose. He didn't have to.

He knew.

She stopped up ahead of him to look in a window. Had to be checkin' herself out, Ray-Ray knew, because there wasn't a shop open on this block, or the next one. The club was one of the only things open, because the people in the neighborhood were trying to hold on, and it seemed one of the things they weren't gonna let go of as easy as the banks, or the post office, or the Chinese cleaners, or the last pizza joint. No, if it wasn't a check cashing 'front or a Church's or a liquor store, it didn't have much chance of survivin' down this way. The club stood out, because people wouldn't let go as easy. Funny about that, thought Ray-Ray, 'cause it was the club he was usin' to get his jack with the Thugs. If it wasn't for the club, he wouldn't have known about Jada, wouldn't have known she'd be leaving, right around four, alone, as always.

Ray-Ray held back, feeling his feet hit the pavement slow and easy, feeling everything draining away as he passed the window where Jada had stopped. Nothing inside but some old flyers behind the dusty, taped windows. Maybe she was prettyin' up, know'd he was comin'. Ray-Ray felt a bounce in his step, knew that he was a-ight. Knew Kennedy would feel confident if he could see him now, knew he wasn't gonna fuck up.

Big pimpin'... he thought, humming to himself, *Everything be different come tomorrow*

Tomorrow, he'd have a Thugs jacket on, and the whole neighborhood would be his. All the respect be his, soon. Everybody'd see, word would get around.

They'd all know.

All he had to do was this.

Halfway up the next block, Ray-Ray caught up to her. He was walking in the street, singing out loud, trying to get her attention while not trying to look like it. He was singin' the latest Jay-Z tune. It turned her head.

"Hey, baby—you walking home all alone?" he asked her. She didn't stop, but slowed to look at him. He was glad he'd ditched the cigarette, stuffed his hands into his pockets. He thought it made him look more easygoing. Trustworthy, almost.

She didn't answer him. They walked in silence a few more steps.

"You wan' me to walk withcha for a few blocks? I'm only goin' to one-two-five, but I'll walk with ya that far, if ya want." he offered. He looked her over. She was a shade darker than Jell-O chocolate pudding, and her skin was as creamy and smooth. Ray-Ray could hear Bill Cosby making gooey slurping noises in his head, and it brought a smile to his face. Jada picked up on it, and couldn't help but smile back. She was wearing a dress, knee-length, and Ray-Ray checked out her legs as he stepped up onto the curb.

"A-ight," she said, nodding approval as she looked him over. "I'm on 'hundred twenty-third."
Didn't matter to him.
He knew.
And they weren't going that far.

"Here, we'll cut up here and catch the Avenue," Ray-Ray said, and she followed him blindly behind a fenced-in lot facing the back of what used to be a department store. Even Ray-Ray couldn't remember the name, it had been that long since it'd gone belly-up and become a few-hundred-thousand-square-foot pigeon coop and crackhouse. Company that didn't mind each other. Tomorrow, even the crackheads and the pigeons would know. Ray-Ray laughed.

"What's so funny?" Jada asked, navigating over a broken slab of concrete and some broken bottles. Twenty five feet, and Ray-Ray would be where he had to be. A step away from the gaping wound in the building that had once been the truck bay.

"Ahhhh, nuthin'," he said back, reaching out to take one of her hands to help her. Without Ray-Ray, she never would have taken the short-cut. He knew it, had counted on it. But it would definitely make the trip shorter. It was almost over now.

"You laughin' at me?" Jada asked, defiantly, dropping his hand and standing on a boulder-sized, upturned piece of blacktop and concrete.

"No, sugar, I ain't laughin' at you. What you think I'm laughin' at you for?" He kept walking. She'd follow. She didn't want to be left here, not alone.

"Well, what you laughin' at, then?" she asked, running a few steps to catch up, careful of where she stepped. She was looking down at her feet, having just crunched down on a piece of broken bottle, when she felt the searing pain in her cheek. Before she could bring her hand to her face to see if she'd been cut, her eyes blurred and swam with tears, and her tongue tasted blood. Her own blood. She wanted to step back, but she was unsteady, and it was getting harder to see. She didn't know if she was going to be able to stand up. She looked to Ray-Ray for help, and felt his shoulder support her as she doubled over.

He was lifting her up, he was going to carry him home, she began to think. But then, as her head cleared just enough, she knew that wasn't right. He wouldn't be picking her up to carry her home.

Not after he'd punched her in the face and stood there watching her, hand balled up in a fist, blood on his knuckles. She tried to say something but her whole head felt as if it were broken. Her tongue was swollen, and it was hard to breathe. She watched the ground as Ray-Ray carried her into the old Alexander's department store, where her mama used to work when her daddy was still alive. She didn't have to touch her cheek to know she'd been cut.

She could see a trail of her blood dripping behind them, as it started to get darker and darker.

Malcolm had started it all, when he came back from doing three for the B&E and hooked up with Kennedy. Kennedy was doing some nickel and dime dealing down in the parks for Big Papa, like most of the unorganized street dealers would. When Malcolm got back, he'd learned some stuff on the inside, and he put it to work for him. One day Big Papa stopped supplying all his small-timers and Malcolm had his crew working the parks, and the streets, and the clubs, and everywhere else. Pretty soon he was spendin' cheese like mad and that's when the Thugs started walkin' the streets. Bad ass niggaz who didn't give a shit and didn't let anybody fuck with 'em. Pablo was part 'Rican and he came up with the design, the chains wrapped around a bloody fist and the crazy, Nazi writin' stylin' the leather. BRUTAL above the fist and THUGS on the bottom. Pretty soon, there wasn't nobody left to say nothin', nobody left to challenge Malcolm's crew.

Everybody knew. So they knew better.

Ya'll gonna make me lose my mind, up in here, up in here

Ray-Ray rolled Jada off his shoulder and she hit the hard ground with a thud. The back of her head banged hard against the cracked concrete, and she tried to sit up, drawing another right hand. This one split her lip wide, and drove her head down again, hard. It didn't sound quite right hitting the concrete. Her hair, damp and matted with blood, had softened the sound. Ray-Ray peeled off his shirt, showing off the tattoo on his right breast, a hand-done black X that she couldn't have focused on even if he hadn't hit her again. It didn't matter, it would be over soon. The he'd have the Thugs jack, and the respect. That's what it was all about, gettin' the respect. All he had to do was finish this thing, bring back the trophy, get the jack.

In, out, be done, be back.

Y'all gonna make me go all out, up in here, up in here

Ray-Ray tore Jada's dress right down the middle, exposing her bra and panties. He threw it to the side, wasn't like she was gonna wanna wear it again all ripped up like that. He watched her eyes swim in her head, watery, rollin' around like a doll's.

He unzipped his pants.

"What you want in for, nigga? You ain't never wanted none o' this shit before?" It's Kennedy's voice. The day he'd confronted Ray-Ray about hanging around so much.

"What you think, man? Be a 'Thug, a-ight? Ain't that what it's all about?"

"Mutherfucka, you wanna be a 'Thug? What the fuck makes you think you got that in you? What you ever done makes you think you kin run with this crew?"

"What you supposed to do? You ain't gonna do nuthin' on your own, not in this town, not to get noticed, get respect. Not with Malcolm on top. You tell me, Kennedy, what'm I s'posed to do but come around, get tight with you, see what

I gotta do earn my way in?"

"Aw, man...Double-R this ain't about schoolyard shit and all that. You come in with the 'Thugs and you in deep, all the way in mutherfucka deep. That what you want? You sure that's what you want?"

"Yeah, 'course that's what I want. You think I'm comin' 'round here wastin' y'all mutherfucka's time an' shit? Wastin' my time? Fuck, it's about respect, and gettin' me some, K, you should know all 'bout that."

Time between them. Silent time. Ray-Ray wasn't sure Kennedy was gonna budge. Wondered if Kennedy didn't want Ray-Ray in for some reason. Maybe they couldn't be friends again. Maybe K thought Ray-Ray would drift and wouldn't have his back when it came down to it. Or maybe something else
a warning
like being jealous. Maybe thinking Ray-Ray would shine. Maybe thinkin' Ray-Ray would outperform all the other niggaz in his class. Outshine 'em all.

But Kennedy budged.

"You come down with me, next week. We go talk to Malcolm and we see. But you better be ready, Ray-Ray. You show up next week, that's it, a-ight? You better be ready to walk the walk, 'cause there ain't gonna be no talkin'."

"I hear you," Ray-Ray agreed, holding out a fist. Kennedy rapped his own on top and Ray-Ray responded in kind.

"Next week," Kennedy said again, walking away.
One last chance...
"Next week. Peace-out, G."

Kennedy just kept on walking.

She opened her mouth, but nothing was coming out but some drool and the occasional grunt. Ray-Ray grabbed her chin in his fist and squeezed. Her lips parted, and he could see where several teeth were hanging from her gums at harsh angles. Only one had disappeared completely. He didn't know if it had fallen out along the way
She had swallowed it
but it didn't matter. He was surprised at how easy the teeth had come loose in her head. How easy it had been to get her here, to keep her quiet. Not that it would matter much now. Here in the depths of the truck bay nobody would hear a thing. He almost wanted her to scream now, wanted to hear her crying out for him to stop, for him to let her go, for mercy. Anything.

The silence was unexpected.

It made him uneasy.

He reached down between her legs, felt her panties. Damp in his hands. Soaked, in fact. He wondered if it was her sweat from the club, or if she had had an idea what he wanted to do with her, if she had had an idea that she'd feel
She had wet herself in fear
what he'd want her to feel.

Why didn't she make any noise?
Ray-Ray tore off her piss-stained panties and rolled them into a ball and *She was supposed to be screaming by now.* stuffed them into her mouth. Her head was tilted to the side, and he could hear her snuffling through her nose, trying to breathe.
Where's the noise? Why isn't she fighting more?
He puller her legs apart roughly, although she lay there as pliant as a rag doll. He could picture Malcolm, watching this, watching him follow-through on his initiation rite and approving. He could see DJ-Kix, turning up the boom box and laying down a playa's track, just for him. Baby-D and Razz and Pearl and all them other hater's watchin' him do it up, watch him earn the 'Thug jack and everything that came with it. Most of all he could see Kennedy, standing like he was right there in the dim truck bay, looking down on Double-R with those cold, dead eyes.
You in all the way now, Double-R. You in deep, all the way in mutherfucka deep.
Ray-Ray was in, could feel her giving way, lubricated by a mix of sweat and urine and her bloody saliva, dribbling down the head of his dick. The roughness of her broken teeth had scratched his cock, so he'd decided to finish the job right.
what have you seen, Kennedy?
what you seen that made your eyes that way?
But he wouldn't ask.
After today, he wouldn't have to.

Cherise was standing in the hallway, waiting for him. He was late, intentionally so, but not so late that he'd make her miss her bus if she was really gonna go. When he stepped inside, she looked at him, exasperated.

"You didn't think I'd wait any longer, did you?"

"Hey, I was caught up, I'm sorry I'm late. It's not like you hafta go or anything."

"Don't you start shit now, Ray, not now. You wanna stay here in this shithole, I can't make you leave. You wanna let this place drag you down, well, fine. I'm not, though. I'm not going to stay here and watch."

"Man, you always talkin' like you're so much better than this place, whatchu gotta be like that for, Cherise?"

Because she was
And he knew it

"Ray, you're my brother, and I love you. But I'm going to go and catch that bus and there's no stopping that. And next week, there's another bus. And the week after that, there's another. And another, and another, until they burn down the goddamned bus station. If you're smart, you'll get on one before it's too late."

"Yeah, well, maybe I'll just get some fly wheels and drive me on up to *Rhode Island* be wit' you and Gram," he laughed.
Knowing she was right
Knowing she was always right
    She reached out, impulsively, wrapping her arms around him. This was it, he knew. She wasn't going to change her mind after all. He hugged her back, weakly. He hadn't expected her to actually leave. To leave him.
    "You get up there any way you can, Ray. You just get out of here, before it's too late."
    And that was it. She grabbed her single suitcase and walked out the door. He didn't try and follow, didn't offer to carry her bag to the bus station for her. She understood. As the bus pulled away, she could picture him there, in the ratty hallway on 125th, just as he could picture her, sitting on the bus in a window seat, not waving good-bye to the cesspool they lived in.
    He promised himself then, that that would be the last time he would ever cry.

He let his full weight rest on her, noticing something on her panties but not paying too much attention. She was tight, and he'd be finished in a few minutes, and then he could get out of here and get back to the crib, turn in his trophy and be handed that 'Thug leather with the paint on the back still so fresh he'd be able to smell it. And tomorrow, when he woke up, everybody'd know.
    Something struck him on the cheek as he got ready to finish, wet and thick. He slowed, then felt it again. And again when he thrust, until he had to pull back and support himself on his arms.
    Her nose, it had come from her nose. He pulled out of her roughly, her blood staining his cock. He clawed at the lumpy mass on his face, repulsed by the feel, and then the smell.
    Vomit...he recognized...she was vomiting through her nose on him!
    The anger welled up inside him. It wasn't supposed to be like this.
where were the screams?
the panties were supposed to be to stop the screams
    He reared back, watched in slow-motion as the toe of the Adidas swung forward and drove into her ribs. Jada could barely move
Her skull was fractured
but instinct rolled her halfway onto her side, where her small, frail arms tried to cover her naked body.
    Ray-Ray reared back again, this time coming down on her
Her brain was swelling
side with his heel. The splintery sound of ribs cracking reverberated in his ears.
    The panties, and nostrils clogged with vomit, had all but caused her to stop breathing
    Ray-Ray could feel Kennedy's eyes on him, could feel his stare. He raised his

foot again, seeking out another target
what have you seen, Kennedy?
what you seen that made your eyes that way?
bringing his foot down on the side of her head, feeling it give, but not all the way.
Both her lungs had been punctured
She was drowning in her own blood
A second time, and he could feel something shift, could feel her head going lopsided as it was caught between his foot and the concrete
Suffocating on her own vomit
And then it was finished. She quivered, spasmed once after he brought both feet down squarely on the side of her head, and then stopped moving altogether.
Ray-Ray looked down, saw her blood coating his sneakers
wouldn't matter, $135 Nikes tomorrow
felt the breath suddenly coming in desperate gasps, as if he'd forgotten to breathe, as if he'd stopped breathing and almost forgot how to start again.
He stepped back, reached for his shirt, felt his body bathed in sweat, felt it oozing thick like oil from his pores. He reached for her dress to try and soak it up, but it didn't do any good. It just kept coming, flowing like a river. His heart felt like it didn't want to slow down, either.
She was dead. No doubt. Her head was half flat.
He pulled on his shirt, tossed the tattered dress aside on a pile of old skids. There was a spot behind them where he'd hide her.
He'd killed her. Like Kennedy had told him to.
She probably wouldn't be found for months. Wouldn't be any investigation, wouldn't be any DNA testing, wouldn't be anything left by then
rats would make sure of that
for anybody to find.

He dragged her body back behind the cobweb-covered wood. He grabbed her by one foot, so that he wouldn't have to touch her where she'd bled or where she'd shit herself. The stench rising in the truck bay was awful, worse than anything he'd ever experienced, and he felt himself gagging, starting to lose control.
Ray-Ray turned, and made to leave. He suddenly felt sick to his stomach. He didn't think he'd make it to fresh air without throwing up. He was halfway there, could see the fading light coming through the bay. He could just make out the fence in the distance, across the jagged, broken up lot.
And then he had to turn around. Bile rising in his throat, he made his way back. He crawled behind the skids, trying to hold his breath all the way, feeling his knee slide in what must have been blood or shit or vomit, and reached out towards her lumpy, misshapen face. He could still make out something on the balled up wad in her mouth, but he closed his eyes so he wouldn't have to look

into hers.
He couldn't believe he had almost done this.
He'd almost left the trophy behind.

They were all still there when he walked in. He'd gone to change his clothes; his pants, shirt and sneakers were all in separate garbage cans behind three different buildings he'd passed on his way to the crib. Kennedy was sitting in a chair across from Malcolm, while the others milled about. Baby-D and Razz were shadowboxing. Kix had on a track Ray-Ray didn't recognize, but it grooved.

"In, out, deed's done, now I's back."

Kennedy was the first over. He reached out, and Ray-Ray dropped the balled up panties in his hand. Kennedy wrinkled his nose up at the stench, then looked Ray-Ray hard in the eyes. He recognized Ray-Ray's were different.

They were cold, dead.

He'd done it, all right. He was in deep, all the way in mutherfucka deep. Kennedy let a slow, narrow smile cross his face. Ray-Ray didn't respond. He was in now, he knew it.

They all did.

Malcolm stepped up and slapped his bear-paw hands down on Ray-Ray's shoulders.

"Pablo," he bellowed. "Bring the man his new threads."

As if the only 'Rican in the crew had miraculously appeared at Malcolm's command, conjured like a genie, he stood behind Ray-Ray and slipped the still-stiff leather jacket onto Double-R's outstretched arms. Ray-Ray worked his shoulders, taking in the feel, the scent of the new leather. He was right, he could still smell the paint, it was that fresh. Malcolm put his hands back on Ray-Ray's shoulders.

"You almost there, Double-R, you just hang on a little longer, you be a full-fledged 'Thug." Ray-Ray looked up, then towards Kennedy. Malcolm's hands clasped down on Ray-Ray's shoulders hard, and then he saw it coming. A flash in Kennedy's hand and the knife was out and driving through the leather just under Ray-Ray's left arm. The knife went through the stiff cowhide like it was paper, and Ray-Ray felt the sting of the blade as it broke through his skin.

Ray-Ray clutched at where Kennedy had stabbed him, feeling the pain spread out from the center of the wound as a warm, wet circle stained his shirt. He looked up into Malcolm's eyes, and didn't have to voice his question.

"Easy, Double-R. My brother barely nicked you. Every 'Thug breaks in his jack with a little sweat, a little blood. You gonna be just fine. I'm gonna send the boys to take you out on the town tonight. Show off the newest member of my bad ass crew. You gon' have the time of your life, a-ight?"

"A-ight."

"What time is it?" asked Double-R, sitting in the back of the Mercedes, holding some tissues against the still-oozing cut Kennedy had put in him so he wouldn't bleed on the interior.

"'Most six, man, why, you hungry? I could go for some Church's, myself," said Kix, riding shotgun.

"Church's sounds good, good idea." But he was no longer paying attention. Outside the tinted windows, the neighborhood, what was left of it, was passing by, and Ray-Ray had never felt more out of place. The check cashing place drifted into the background and his eyes lazily followed it. The liquor store, with it's usual crowd of characters standing out front, didn't seem familiar at all. And when they stopped at a light, Ray-Ray couldn't bring his eyes to look at the club.

There was a crowd of people milling about. Women, all of them.

Couldn't stomach seeing the club's facade, the big sign above the doors *Looking concerned. One of them pointing in one direction, one in another.* with the big clover with the hand-painted Hs in each of the leaves *Some of the women were holding hands, one of them was crying, another was speaking into a cell-phone, her face frantic and worried* or the smiley faces, and the girls walking hand-in-hand-in hand in a chain.

The club was one of the only things open, because the people in the neighborhood were trying to hold on

Tomorrow, Ray-Ray knew, it would be different all over. For him, for the neighborhood

The club was one of the things they weren't gonna let go of as easy

for the club, for everybody. Tomorrow there'd be another baller rolling the streets. Tomorrow there'd be another playa to deal with

Eventually, a police car would come, but the officer would probably be white, probably wouldn't take a good report, probably wouldn't put in a report until a day had gone by...maybe longer

and the 'Thugs would be one bad-ass big baller stronger.

The club stood out, because people wouldn't let go as easy.

And the neighborhood would be upset about the lack of police action, and wonder how a seven year old girl could just disappear into thin air on her way home.

"Hey, lookit' *those*."

Ray-Ray opened his eyes, followed Kix's finger to the storefront window. Through the security gates he could see exactly what Kix was pointing at.

"Tomorrow," Ray-Ray said, closing his eyes.

"Man, wonder what those babies go for?"

"$135," said Ray-Ray.

Not that it made a difference.

COVEN

"You really should join us, Catherine. It would make all of us *so* much happier if you'd come."

"Well, you know, Adele, I think it would just be better if I didn't, I really wouldn't feel...*comfortable*." Adele's lips pursed, just for a brief second, before shifting to a broad smile. Catherine stiffened, it was as if somebody had flipped a switch, and Adele had shifted into another mode of personality.

"Well, if you do reconsider..." Adele added, wheeling her cart towards the canned goods. Catherine watched her turn the corner, and breathed a hard sigh of relief. Her elbow came to rest on the handle of her shopping cart, and her eyes fluttered closed as she tried to erase Adele from her mind.

"We do hope you change your mind!" called Adele, leaning back into view. Catherine managed a smile in return, her hands clenched too tightly to return the gesture. Finally, with a bob of her head, Adele disappeared, this time for good, somewhere off beyond frozen foods.

Catherine continued to look over her shoulder every few minutes as she unloaded her cart in the Kroger's parking lot. She was wary, not only of Adele Kerrigan, but of any of the other town women who were involved with Adele and the circle of friends which formed her semi-social clique. A stiff fall breeze was picking up, and fallen, multicolored leaves bristled against Catherine's bare ankles. Even her wool half-coat wasn't enough to protect her from the chills dancing up the full length of her spine. The weather wasn't the only thing that was turning the air chilly, that much she could feel. Her only goal aside from getting the full week's worth of groceries home was to avoid any further impromptu meetings and their inevitable delays. Daniel would be home from school in a while, and she meant to be back at the house well before the bus dropped him off. A meeting-up with Adele Kerrigan, even for the briefest of moments, was more than enough for one week.

It took the old '78 GMC three good cranks before finally turning over, and Catherine made a mental note to have Simpson down at the garage give the spark plugs a check. The '78 was sorely due for some preventative maintenance, and if Catherine could scrape together the necessary money for an oil change and tune-up, she vowed that she would. She could think of fewer scenarios worse than being stuck in West Barlow without personal transportation.

Half a mile from Kroger's, the veritable center of town, Catherine finally began to feel the knot in her gut loosen, the tension starting to dissipate. The sense of nausea that had overcome her when she had been forced to confront Adele Kerrigan mid-way between paper goods and pet foods was ebbing.

Regardless of how ridiculous it seemed, Adele had an effect on Catherine that she was embarrassed to admit. Adele frightened Catherine, and no matter how strong Catherine tried to be when facing the woman, she knew that Adele was well aware of the fact that she put Catherine on edge. If she didn't outright know that she frightened Catherine, she must have had a good idea of just how unnerved she made her. Ever since Joe's death, five months earlier, Catherine felt a bizarre sort of peer pressure being placed upon her, as Adele and several of the other women of Barlow tried to recruit her into their group of . . .

Of what? Catherine couldn't place a finger on it. From what she'd been told, or from what she had pieced together on her own, Adele was the ringleader of a group of, basically, busybodies. These particular busybodies, however, included most—if not all—of the wives of the most important men in town. Sure, there were rumors, how these women had enough power to influence the zoning board, get the auxiliary police to ticket homeowners who let their lawns grow too high, or their music play too loud. Children called them the old witches, telling tall tales about séances and rituals carried out on the nights of the full moon. They were women who staunchly supported a 9:00 P.M. curfew on Halloween night, and for that they would forever draw the ire of children who lived to spend October 31st clad in costume, going door-to-door and trick-or-treating. Of course, none of the homes Adele and her friends lived in were targets of children seeking candy. Everybody knew who was counted among Adele's group, and those houses—all a waste of precious pre-9:00 trick-or-treat time—were skipped by all. Yet for all of the exaggerated versions of what really went on, or the agenda of that inner circle, a shred of truth seemed to come through. Catherine sometimes wondered if she was the only person in West Barlow who felt the same way about Adele and her nosy friends. She shrugged for the benefit of no one but herself, and nosed the GMC out of the thin traffic on Mount Aspen

Road, and onto one of the smaller, nameless veins which led out of town proper, and into the small hills that formed the West Barlow suburbs.

Watching the woods pass by on either side of her, Catherine decided that today would be a fine enough day to take Daniel and Tranis out in the field to play ball. The thought of her son running about in his red winter jacket, with the big, lumbering German shepherd chasing behind, brought a warm smile to her face, the first to grace her lips all day. In fact, had she not been forced to practically overturn the GMC an eyeblink later, she truly believed that it might have been turning into a good day after all.

The image horrified her. Cutting the wheel of the GMC hard to the right, she just barely avoided Claire Dougherty, while at the same time veering so far toward the shoulder that the right front tire of the GMC caught loose gravel and then nothing. There was a second of feeling weightless, followed by the vehicle pitching violently up and forward, then down into the drainage ditch.

Catherine felt the soft padding of the steering wheel first, before the solid plastic beneath stopped her head from going any further. Her teeth ripped into her bottom lip, and the warm coppery taste of blood filled her mouth. Her eyes teared and her mind swam, while the strains of a Paula Cole tune faded off into the background. Everything grew fuzzy as the GMC lurched to a halt, just shy of a cluster of trees, their black skin dull and lifeless before her.

In a moment, it became painfully obvious to Catherine that the blow had been too harsh for her to simply shrug off. She didn't know where Claire Dougherty was now, she just hoped it was far away. The struggle to lift her head and get the GMC started up again was enough to have her on the verge of blacking out, and she had to stop and take a breath between efforts. She wondered if she might have suffered a concussion. Her stomach was doing flip-flops and her chest seemed to heave with each breath, making the decision not to try and overexert herself a no-brainer. It was easy enough to slowly gather her thoughts, to formulate a plan while sitting there with her head resting against the imitation leather steering wheel cover. She would have to wait until the groggy, drugged feeling subsided enough for her to get the GMC, which had stalled in the commotion, running again.

"Does it hurt much, Catherine?" came a voice, cutting through some of the haziness.

"Who is that? I need some help. Can you give me a hand?" asked Catherine. It was difficult for her to gauge just how much time had passed, and the voice sounded so far away that she couldn't tell whether or not it was that of Claire Dougherty. Clarity returned briefly. Catherine wanted no part of Claire Dougherty. In fact, she wanted to turn the key and gun the GMC to life and barrel home like a bat out of hell.

"There is no running, Catherine." came the voice, making itself heard once more. Catherine swallowed hard, feeling her senses begin to return. It was sobering—for a moment she actually imagined that whoever was speaking had been able to read her mind. Long silence followed. There had been no voice, of that she was sure. She had been projecting as she floated in and out of consciousness. She had a concussion, of that she was sure, and she had to move the GMC. The image of driving the GMC hell-bent out of town, with Daniel and Tranis playfully roughhousing in the back seat, returned, and she couldn't deny that the vision seemed like paradise.

Her hands gripped the steering wheel, sticky with coagulating blood, but Catherine managed to push herself back against the bucket seat and get her bearings. She could feel more blood drying in her hair, making it cling to her cheeks and neck. Her eyes were red and puffy, and she looked like she had been backhanded across the mouth, but she could focus on her own image in the rear-view and not see double, and that made her breathe a sigh of relief.

"Where are you?" she demanded hoarsely, "Where are you, Claire? Where the hell did you go?"

The reply came in the form of a whistle of wind through the trees, and nothing more.

"Fine then..." Catherine spat, gripping the key to the GMC and turning it sharply in the ignition. "Fuck you, you bitch," she muttered, feeling the engine roar to life. Her neck cracked as she turned to look back over her shoulder, reversing the GMC once again onto the road. The dash clock, which hadn't worked in years, offered no clue as to how long she'd been off the road. By the way the sky was looking, she estimated that she'd been in the ditch for the better part of an hour, which worried her more than her condition and appearance. Over an hour. That meant that Daniel would be coming home soon from school.

"*Damnit*," she muttered under her breath. It would be a contest to see who arrived home first. She didn't want Daniel to see her the way she looked, or to have to explain the accident to a more-than-curious seven-year-old. Again, the idea of leaving West Barlow played in her mind, this time for good. Several times she had considered it during the past months, especially as fall grew colder and winter loomed. The house in West Barlow had been in Joe's family for generations, so far back that even he didn't know its full history. What made matters worse was that Joe's will stipulated that she never sell the house or the property, that the family legacy never be transferred, except on to family. It was the way it had always been done, and Joe, following the tradition, had bound her to by the chain as well. Joe's death had come suddenly, leaving her ill-prepared to bring up Daniel and without many possibilities. There was no way she could afford to go anywhere without being able to rid herself of the big Victorian at the end of Wyndham Road. With her own parents dead, and Joe's parents unwilling to even speak to her since the wedding, she was alone, pathetically alone, in the odd New England town. Still, as she had been thinking more and more as of late, just because she couldn't sell the place didn't mean she and Daniel had to live in it...or in West Barlow for that matter. Perhaps renting it would be the solution. Or maybe Joe's parents would give her something for it—assuming of course they would deign to speak with her. Maybe there was something she could work out, maybe something through her attorney...

"Oh, no!" she said aloud. All the wind rushed out of her. Coming towards her, already two stops past Wyndham Road, was the old, yellow school bus. It struck her like a bolt of lightning that there would be nobody home for Daniel, and that he had no key. Her foot pressed down against the accelerator, and the GMC responded with a loud upshift in gears, a puff of blue smoke belched from the tailpipe. It was only a few blocks, she tried to assure herself, he would wait at the front door for her, listening to Tranis' fervent barks and watching his tail wagging through the window. He would wait, she knew he would wait. She hoped he would wait. She pressed the accelerator flat to the floorboard.

Swinging wide into the driveway, Catherine tore out the rose bush she and Joe had planted upon their arrival in Barlow, fifteen months earlier. She leapt from the cab, leaving the GMC running, the door hanging ajar. "Oh, no, no..."

"Daniel!" she cried, running up the walk and through the open front door. It was freezing in the foyer, and there was no response from Daniel, if indeed he was inside.

"Oh, God, *DANIEL!*" Where was he? And where was Tranis? Catherine shuddered at the thought that something had happened to the hulking shepherd, because it would mean that Daniel had been left unprotected. It also would have meant that something extraordinary had overcome the big dog, rightfully deserving of the name Daniel had tried to bestow on it when he was four. She remembered the day Joe had brought the big dog home, still a pup but already a menacing size. It had taken an instant liking to Daniel, and the boy, awed by the size of the shepherd's teeth, had named him on the spot—Tranis, the young boy's best attempt at Tyrannosaurus .

But where were they *now*? Catherine had searched practically the entire upstairs, and still there was no sign of the boy or the dog. Panic began to set in as Catherine ran from room to room, frantically calling out their names.

And then she saw them. From the hallway window, she could see the two standing side by side out in the backyard, staring at something in the grass.

"Daniel! Daniel!" she called, slapping her palm against the glass before foolishly realizing that there wasn't any way they could hear her from where they were standing. She turned and flew down the steps, throwing open the back door hard enough to warp the metal frame and screen as she ran out to take her son into her arms. She hugged him with all her strength, forgetting the pain in her lips and neck, or the blood drying on her skin. She was happy, overjoyed to hold her son in her arms and hear the sounds of Tranis alternately barking and whining beside them.

"Oh, Danny, I'm sorry I wasn't here for you, I was so worried, you two had me so—"

"Mom," Daniel interrupted, his voice shaky.

"What, honey?" Catherine asked, smoothing the boy's hair back with her hand.

"What does that mean?" asked the boy, pointing to the spot he had been staring at.

Catherine screamed.

The message which had been left in the grass was unmistakable. Carved into the base of a big elm were three small characters—obviously meant to represent Tranis, Daniel and herself. The three were depicted standing beneath a large tree icon—unmistakably the mammoth oak which stood in the West Barlow Courthouse yard. Catherine was well aware of the legends associated with that tree, and to think that they had been ordered to appear before it, was more than enough incentive for her. Her decision had been made. She would get some things together and get the hell out of Barlow. It was already late afternoon, and the darkness which was falling seemed to offer the perfect cover under which she and her family would slip out of town.

At Interstate 34, the first sign of trouble appeared. She met up with road construction, and the leering face of Mel Thompson, Ella Thompson's husband. He offered her an alternate route, but it was one that was both time-consuming and out of the way. She left him smiling and shrugging his shoulders after asking if the road would be passable before morning. Daniel was sleeping beside her. Tranis was sitting with his head out the passenger window, tongue flapping in the breeze.

She thanked Mel, hoping it didn't sound as false as it felt, and nosed the GMC around the detour cones and back the way she'd come.

Sheriff Kerrigan himself met her at the junction between Old Mill Road and Sunrise Highway. Catherine waited for the explanation—it seemed that a tree had fallen, knocking down some power lines, Kerrigan explained to her—and it became painfully obvious to her that there would be no leaving West Barlow tonight. At least, not in the GMC.

"Ed, is there any way out of town that's open? I'm supposed to be visiting my in-laws tonight." Catherine tried, hoping for a positive reply.

"Well, now, Catherine, I've got to say that no, I don't think there is...Why don't you turn around and take the boy for a picnic, or something, maybe down at the courthouse. There's a little going-on set for tonight, and I bet you'd all be welcome to come."

"I don't think so, Ed." Catherine spat, putting the GMC in reverse and leaving Kerrigan in her dust. Ed watched the GMC disappear up the road, through the cloud of settling dust.

"And you don't talk to your in-laws either, Catherine."

When Simpson pulled down the **CLOSED** sign just as she nosed the GMC into the station, Catherine knew that there would be no avoiding a showdown at the courthouse. It was already past six o'clock, and the GMC, which had been on the go all day, barely had fumes left to run on. It began to sputter and stall as she pulled into the only open parking spot in front of the courthouse. The temperature outside was dropping. Whatever was "going-on" out at the courtyard, would have to be over quickly. The grey sky was threatening to open up at any minute, and it could just as easily begin dropping flakes as it could spitting freezing rain on them. Not planning to endure a minute longer than necessary, Catherine woke a groggy, half-asleep Daniel, and locked the GMC. She walked him around the back, Tranis whining his disapproval as they went.

There was a small bonfire burning when she came into view, and a circle of women standing before her, Adele Kerrigan in the center. They were dressed in dark robes, their hair hanging free in the wind. Catherine felt a chill that was unrelated to nature race up her back.

"Catherine," Adele purred, "We *knew* you would come." The others began to move forward, closing in, tightening the circle. Catherine felt the hair on the back of her neck prickling up. Claire, Ella, Maryanne Russo—the leader of the PTA—and even Brenda Walsh from the town council, they were all there.

"What do you want with me?" Catherine asked defiantly. There was a brief pause, and then it began. At first it was just a few giggles, until the women broke into full fledged laughter, as if Catherine had just told the funniest joke they had ever heard. At the fringes of the circle, a few of the town men appeared. Ed Kerrigan, Mel Thompson, Phil Russo, some others Catherine didn't know but recognized by sight.

"You?" asked Adele, drawing two objects from her flowing robe. She shook her head from side to side. In her right hand she held a rope, in her left, a large butcher's knife. "Why, Catherine, you egotist! This isn't about *you*—it was never about you. We've plenty of kindred spirits here, so there's no need to add another...but as you can see," Adele regarded all those around her with a sweep of her arm. "We're all beyond the bearing years, and that, dear, is where you come in...We need a young woman willing to give of *herself*, so that her child might live—among *us!*"

Catherine stepped back, gripped tightly and drawn into the arms of those who would carry her to the big oak. Soon after, her final cries would fade off into the night, carried by the stiff, fall breeze. Her screams of terror and agony would be replaced by the jubilant cries of the group below, as they celebrated the sacrifice of one soul, so that the power of another would be their own.

THE MONTHLY

Ewell Wadkins was not a drunk: he was a good old-fashioned wino. Like the bumbling, stumbling Otis on the old *Andy Griffith Show*, Ewell was a good-hearted, good-natured loaf about town. What made Ewell more palatable was that he wasn't just an alcohol-soaked blight on one of Connors Glen's streets and benches, but instead he was a wino with beliefs.

Like Blanche Dubois, Ewell relied on the kindness of others—albeit not quite strangers. After all, in a town the size of Connors Glen, pop. 1,086, there really weren't enough residents to be strangers for very long. Since Ewell was odd, he did odd jobs. Since he was fat, those who utilized his services usually threw in lunch with the work and wage. A beer usually accompanied that lunch, and the total package made for a mutually beneficial employer-wino relationship, one which kept lawns mowed, loose brush on one's property bundled, and bald tires from piling up at Newman's Gas and Auto—dragged over to the dump where they belonged.

Among Ewell Wadkins' beliefs were the theories that Ronald Reagan didn't suffer from Alzheimer's, but instead had been kidnapped by aliens so that he could go to their home planet and lead them as he had led the US; that if you stood too close to a microwave when it was cooking your food, that it scanned your brain and transmitted information about your eating habits to the company that had produced the food you were cooking; and that dinosaurs had never really existed—it was all a marketing ploy by museums who would have nothing else to show or sell to stay in business. Ewell had plenty of others, but these were among his favorite and most thought-out. Spontaneous human combustion was something he was still wrestling with, but laser-mounted spacecraft was a distinct possibility. Ewell Wadkins was no believer in NASA, or in any attempt to try to fly off the floating marble inhabited by human beings.

Though widely regarded as harmless, Ewell was no stranger to the Connors Glen police station. Five full-timers and two part-timers comprised the Connors Glen police force, and at one time or another each of the public servants had driven Ewell to the trailer he called home, or had allowed him to sleep off a particularly bountiful evening of imbibing in one of the three cells the building housed. So, while seeing Ewell at the station was nothing new, for Gail Tasker, seeing Ewell all worked up in a lather and demanding to see Sheriff Shaw at the ungodly hour of 8:30 a.m. was one for the books.

Behind the animated Ewell, senior deputy Russell Cobb was twirling his index finger by his temple. Gail was trying to ignore Cobb, difficult as it was in small quarters. Of course, Ewell was oblivious to Cobb's gesticulations behind him as he pleaded his case to the female deputy. So far, she had been able to gain little information from Ewell who, surprisingly, didn't completely reek of gin.

"Ewell, calm down and start from the beginning," Gail tried again with the agitated wino. Instead, Ewell shook his head violently, and repeated his original demand.

"Miss Tasker, I told you, I need to speak to the Sheriff, right now. I seen something awful and I have to tell him right away." Ewell wiped his sweaty forehead with the back of a meaty palm. "Please," he tried, "I really need to talk to the sheriff."

"Ewell, the Sheriff will be here in a few minutes, but there's no reason that you can't tell myself and deputy Cobb what you saw while we wait for him together." Gail was sympathetic. The more Ewell pleaded, the more emphatic he became. Gail knew, as did Cobb, that likely Ewell had seen something all right—something along the lines of a hallucination or perhaps he'd experienced a bout of night terrors. Still, at this hour and this coherent, she wondered.

"No, no, no," Ewell responded, his frustration level—and his voice—rising. The change in pitch caught Cobb's attention. He was watching Ewell more closely now, beginning to consider and evaluate the wino. None of them had ever considered Ewell a threat before, but with Ewell's extensive alcohol abuse history it had come up between them more than once. What if one day Ewell simply lost it? What if the drunk with the good heart one day snapped and lost control? Who knew what Wadkins might be capable of, given the chance. Cobb had never been as sympathetic as others to Ewell, but even he doubted among them that Ewell had it in his make-up to actually do the kinds of things one saw on the news. Kidnap a child...rape one of the old women who supplied him with temporary employment and a hot meal. Still, as he heard Ewell's voice rising—something none of them had ever experienced before—concern began to creep in.

"Ewell," Gail tried "Why don't you take a deep breath and relax. There's no reason to get upset, deputy Cobb and I will—"

"Aw, horseshit! Cobb is back there behind makin' crazy signs with his hands, I know what he thinks of me. Please, ain't you got a radio or something you can raise the Sheriff on? Get him to hurry?"

Gail shot a glance to the surprised Cobb. Neither of them had ever heard Ewell utter a profanity in their midst, and Cobb was left trying to figure out how Ewell had detected his gestures. Cobb still doubted that Ewell would get violent, but he was now leaning on Gail's desk and seemed to be getting a little too close for comfort.

"Now, Ewell, you know I'm just funnin' with you," Cobb offered, walking over and putting two cups of coffee down on the edge of Tasker's desk. He took a wooden seat and turned it backwards, straddling it. "Here, have a cup and we'll give Sheriff Shaw a holler and get to the bottom of this, all right?"

Ewell looked at Gail and then to Cobb. Going back and forth between the two, he tried to gauge whether or not they were telling him the truth, or whether they wanted him to drink the coffee which he suspected Cobb had drugged.

"Please call him. Just give him a jingle and I'll sit down and be calm and even drink your nice coffee. Just give him a jingle, okay? I promise..."

Cobb nodded and Gail pulled the dispatch radio handset. Ewell seemed satisfied with the gesture, and took the cup Cobb held out towards him, although he didn't take a drink. Gail paged Shaw on the two-way, waited, got nothing. This was strange, if Shaw was in his car, he would undoubtedly respond. She smiled thinly and repeated the page. Ewell began to show concern on his face. Cobb watched as Gail tried a third time, unsuccessfully, to raise Shaw on the radio. What had Ewell seen?

"Oh no," Ewell stammered, looking down at the floor. He began to pace nervously in the space in front of Gail's desk. Cobb tried to understand his mumbling and thought he made out the words, "Not him too," and quickly got to his feet.

"Ewell, you tell me now, what is it that you saw, and why do you need Sheriff Shaw so bad? Don't give me any excuses, either, I only want answers." Cobb's tone was harsher than he wanted but he didn't regret it. Now his concern was legitimate, and unless Ewell started to be more forthcoming in his responses, the kid gloves treatment was about to end.

"Once more, please. Just try one more time, okay?"

"Ewell, so help me God, if you don't start talking I am going to—"

The entrance of Sheriff Scott Shaw at the door dropped the rising tension level dramatically. Cobb heard Gail breathe out a deep sigh as the Sheriff entered the station, a box of doughnuts under his arm and a file filled with paperwork under the other.

"What's going on?" he asked, coming towards the pool of desks. "I was just coming around the corner when you radioed. Something wrong? 'Scuse me, Ewell. Help yourself to a doughnut."

"Ewell here's been looking for us to get a hold of you," explained Cobb. "He says he's seen something that you need to know about, but he hasn't told us what it is yet."

"That true, Ewell? There something you need to tell me?" Shaw tossed his Sheriff's baseball cap down on his desk and sat on the corner, facing the man.

"Yes sir," answered Ewell. "But Sheriff, I want to tell you that I didn't have nothing to do with it. I was just walkin', is all, and that's when I saw it. You know I would never do nothin' like this, never. Not hurtin' anybody."

Now the wino had the attention of all three law enforcement officers. Whatever Ewell had seen, or was part of, included somebody getting hurt. Perhaps worse. Shaw read Ewell's body language and his discomfort. Like the others, he didn't believe Wadkins capable of crime more serious than public drunkenness. Now, he wondered if they might have underestimated.

"Who got hurt, Ewell?" questioned Shaw. "And how bad, Ewell? You have to tell me what you saw, so we can help."

"I was cuttin' through the back property, 'cause I got tires to lug up to the dump today," began Ewell, trying to remain composed. "So I wanted to get down there and get an early start. I was taking a shortcut, and that's when I saw the torn screen...and the blood."

"Blood?" asked Cobb. If this was no hallucination, if there was blood and a torn screen on a home in Connors Glen, it would be the first violent crime in nearly 33 years.

"How much blood, Ewell?" asked Shaw solemnly. He knew Wadkins to be a drunk, for sure, but he doubted that if Ewell believed that somebody had only been injured, that he would be taking so much time to let them know about it. The thought left a hollow feeling in the pit of his stomach. He was regretting the Bavarian creme he had smuggled out of the box in the truck on the way over from the bakery.

Ewell was starting to get worked-up again, but this time Gail recognized it as purely emotional. Whatever Ewell had gone through, he was only now beginning to exhibit some of the signs of shock.

"A lot, Sheriff...There was so much blood. And, and...pieces. I only saw pieces, not anybody, just...just pieces." Ewell was sobbing now. He was clutching his face in his hands and bawling like a baby. Tears poured down his round face as he tried to catch enough breath to say more. Gail came around the desk and pushed a chair behind Ewell, who sunk into it.

"Sheriff, I ain't never seen nothing like it...I'm sorry, I'm so sorry," he wailed.

"What are you sorry for, Ewell? Why are you sorry?" Shaw was kneeling in front of the man, looking into Ewell's face where it showed through his pudgy hands.

"Ewell, did you have anything to do with the people who got hurt? You can tell me, it's all right, we'll take care of you here. You're okay, you're with friends. Did you have anything to do with anybody getting hurt?"

Ewell shook his head violently in the negative. "No sir," he denied. "I couldn't ever hurt no one. It's just, it's—" Ewell was breathing so hard and fast now that he was on the verge of hyperventilating. Gail was standing now. Shaw waited until Ewell's breathing had slowed just enough to ask him another question.

"What is it, Ewell? You can tell me. You know that, right? You can tell me anything." Ewell looked the Sheriff in the eye, and then his head dropped again into his hands as he was wracked with sobs. Shaw was torn up watching the man's emotions pull him apart. And still, inside himself, there was a sense of dread. He knew the area well where Ewell would be making his shortcut. The Bavarian creme in his stomach was rapidly souring.

"Who's hurt, Ewell? Where are the people who are hurt?" Shaw asked, patiently. The answer wrenched his gut like a belly full of buckshot.

"The-the Grove house," Ewell finally blurted out. "They're all gone up at the Grove house..." Gail gasped and took a step back. Cobb swallowed loudly enough for them all to hear as Ewell collapsed back into his chair. Shaw held the arms of Ewell's chair for support as he pulled himself to his feet. He realized that he was sweating profusely now in the well air-conditioned station. He turned to Cobb.

"Get your gear and guns—you ride with me. Gail, you call in the rest of the gang and as soon as you have one of them here to hold the fort, you get up to the Grove house and help us out up there. As soon as we verify what we have, we'll see who needs to be called."

"Sheriff—?"

"Let's go eyeball this for ourselves first, Russell," Shaw interrupted. "When we get there, we'll know. Ewell, why don't you grab a cot at the Hilton and get some rest, all right?" Shaw had been calling Cell 3 the Hilton ever since they had installed a new sink. Ewell had spent many a night in there. Ewell did not respond with anything more than he could—a simple nod acknowledging his agreement. Shaw gestured at Gail to watch Ewell carefully, and patted his belt where his key ring was attached. She got the message and nodded. Ewell was going to the Hilton willingly, but they planned to keep him there until they had some answers. A precaution they had never taken before.

"Let's go," Shaw directed, pulling two shotguns off the wall and handing one to Cobb. Silently, the two walked out of the station, leaving Gail to bring in the others to man things. As she rang Ken Dawe to rouse him, she heard the tires of Shaw's Ford Ranger peeling off down the street to the Grove house. The home where his sister and brother-in-law lived.

The Grove house had stood for more than ninety years, although it had never belonged to a family named Grove, and hadn't been a living quarters until after World War II. In 1912, Leland Meade had developed the land he inherited from his father into apple groves, believing that the newly formed township of Connors Glen would become an agricultural hotbed. What Meade hadn't foreseen when he planted was the First World War, and the Great Depression. By 1930, the Grove house, originally a large cider-pressing barn and office for the failing Meade Apple Grove was abandoned, the apple trees left to their own, and the acreage gradually parcelled out to people who wanted to build homes along the border of the vast forest just to the north of the original grove. After the Second World War, an enterprising veteran bought the old cider barn and remodeled the inside. With fresh white paint and red shutters, the large cider barn was transformed into the Grove house. It had since been through two owners, the most recent of whom was Sheriff Shaw's sister, Vickie and her family: her husband, Walter, and their son Kyle. Driving out to the Grove house was a nearly daily pleasure for the unmarried lawman, as he was a regular at dinner and weekend barbecues.

If Ewell was right, Shaw was driving out to the old house to see if any of his remaining family were still alive. His heart felt like a hot oven brick in his chest. Much as he wanted to believe that Ewell had been having drunken hallucinations, he knew it was untrue. He sped towards the Grove house in silence, Cobb beside him cradling his shotgun, not knowing what, if anything, to say. Once they reached the long, rural stretch of Wilkerson Road, Shaw was pressing the Ranger to the high side of eighty. There were only a few homes out this way, each a good walking distance from the next. Winter snow made snowmobiling to the next-door-neighbors' the preferred means of travel, particularly from the Grove house—it marked the end of Wilkerson Road. Beyond the Grove house was a hundred or so feet of field grass, and then the woods themselves.

The Ranger hit the drive and started kicking up stones and gravel. Where the road ended, they passed a green sign attached to a yellow wooden post. The metal sign bore the distinct outline of a tractor, and the legend: BEYOND HERE YOU BETTER RIDE A DEERE. Shaw remembered when his brother-in-law had come across the vintage sign at a flea market over in Calder County. They had dug the hole with Shaw's post digger the next afternoon while the yellow paint was drying. The memory flooded back as the Ranger's wake left the post and sign coated in dust. The Ranger came to a stop about fifteen feet from the front of the house. Shaw left room for an outdoor perimeter if one was necessary.

"How do you wanna play it, boss?" Cobb asked. Shaw cut the engine, stuffed the keys in his pocket.

"Go around the far outside," Shaw directed, pointing with his finger. "Keep your head down passing the windows, we're not exactly showing up like it's a surprise out here. I'll go up the drive on this side. Ewell says he was using the back way through as a shortcut, means he was coming down from the west. If what he saw was what he saw, we'll know it when we get around back."

"Gotcha," confirmed Cobb, climbing out of the passenger door. Shaw reached into the extended cab portion and retrieved his shotgun, double-checked the load and felt on his hip for his Glock. He gave the nod to Cobb, who had done the same, and the two men began to approach the quiet, white house with the cherry red shutters.

Cobb crouched and scurried past the windows at the front of the house. When he got to the edge of the one closest to the corner, he cautiously stood and peered inside. He'd been a visitor at the Grove house on many an occasion, and knew the layout well. He was looking into Vickie's sewing room, which appeared neat and deserted. He did a quick scan of the room and dropped down again, his back against the house facade. A quick look over to Shaw confirmed the same on the sheriff's end of things. Shaw would have been outside the family's TV room, and when he shook his head at Cobb in the negative, it was a good indication that the front of the house was clear. Shaw jerked his head in the direction he was moving, and signalled silently. Three fingers and then a closed fist. Cobb nodded, acknowledging the thirty second time Shaw was setting for the two men to sweep the side of the house. It was plenty of time, and if either of the two men did not appear within that time frame, it was a silent signal that they had encountered something, trouble or otherwise. Shaw disappeared around the driveway side of the house, and Cobb took a deep breath before turning the corner on his side. Coming off the front of the building, Cobb felt the neck of his shirt sticky against his skin. He was sweating bullets even in the breezy, early-morning air. He found himself scanning the grounds to the east of the Grove house with as much dread as apprehension. The big elm tree with the tractor tire rope swing loomed before him, and just seeing the empty swing hanging motionless sent chills up his sweat-soaked back. The fall leaves had already started abandoning the tree, and the stark, lower branches stood out sharply against the cloudless sky. Cobb rued the silence, wished that sound would come from somewhere; a bird, some squirrels chasing through the grass, anything. He was uncomfortable and his mouth was dry. He found himself praying silently that Ewell had finally gone off the deep end, that perhaps in the wee hours, he had finally taken down the fifth of gin that had killed off one brain cell too many.

    Cobb got a glance into the sewing room from the window at the side of the house, confirmed to himself all was clear, and moved forward. The window dead center on his side of the house was a small frosted glass pane that faced out from the main floor bathroom. Cobb pulled himself up to get as good a look inside as he could. The frosted glass blocked more than half his vision, but he could make out the fuzzy outlines of the shower, sink and commode. He did not see anything that looked like bloodstains; the only noticeable break in the white porcelain and tile an oval blue bath mat on the floor. Satisfied, he moved on towards the back of the house, where Walter kept his office.

    Shaw had made his way around the west side of the Grove house slowly, doing a cursory once-over of his brother-in-law's Bronco before pressing close to the side of the building again and getting a look at what the family room and main floor guest bedroom contained. In each, Shaw saw nothing out of the ordinary. Both rooms appeared to be in order, both rooms exactly as he would have expected to find them had he come by for a dinner or a routine visit. This, however, was anything but a routine visit. The fact that the rooms look undisturbed had done nothing to allay his fears. The house stood eerily silent, long after Vickie and his brother-in-law would have been up. No smell of slab bacon or eggs frying in the kitchen were seeping out to comfort Shaw, no sounds of movement from within or upstairs. The fact that Roscoe, the family's nosy golden retriever hadn't picked up on Shaw's presence had been the most unsettling thing that Shaw had noticed thus far. The six-year-old retriever could tell when Shaw was coming and often bounded out through his doggie door around back to meet the Ranger before Shaw could exit the vehicle. Shaw had given his nephew the dog as a puppy for his eighth birthday. Not hearing Roscoe's barking as he came to the back of the house had set his nerves on edge. His one shoulder against the rear corner of the west end, Shaw paused and took a deep breath. Around the back, he would be moving about ten or so feet to the screened in back porch, the spot where Ewell had been able to look inside and see the carnage he had described at the station house. Steeling himself for whatever he might be faced with, Shaw tightened his grip on the shotgun in his hands, and turned the corner.

    Cobb came around the east corner of the house, dropped into a crouch, and shouldered the shotgun, training it on the back porch. He scanned the wide expanse of yard which ended at the forest treeline, and saw nothing out of the ordinary.

But he smelled something quite different.

It was a sour smell, and it was unmistakably coming from the screened-in porch. Only, as Cobb looked more closely, he could see spots where the porch was no longer screened in. Moving deliberately forward, he could see some of the screens had been compromised. The closer he got, he could also see that what he had initially taken as simply patterns in the mesh were not as they appeared. There were stains—large, dark stains. Stains that were not caused by blocking or reflecting light, but obscuring it completely. Stains that had been left by something thick, and wet. Cobb bit his lip—Ewell had not been lying.

Shaw's eyes fixed on the huge, gaping hole in the main panel of screen. How many nights had he and his sister and brother-in-law sat just behind that screen and watched snow fall, or Kyle racing around with Roscoe and a tennis ball, or a burning leaf pile? Now, the screen had been ripped to shreds, and there was an unmistakable stain down the side of the white, painted back wall that had also stained the dying brown grass a rusty brown. Ewell's terror and shaky voice echoed in Shaw's head. Pieces, the frightened wino had claimed, nothing but pieces...

Shaw's nostrils constricted as he stalked towards the house, shotgun trained on the side door to the porch. He detected Cobb approaching from the east, also with gun at the ready and walking upright. They came around the back, and stood about a dozen feet from one another, surveying the damage.

"There's some blood on the grass, try not to step in any when we move in," said Shaw. Cobb could tell that the Sheriff had gone wooden at what they had found thus far. He let Shaw take the lead as they closed in on the area where it appeared the house had been compromised, the screen with the gaping hole in it.

Shaw was keeping his head tucked in the event that there was somebody inside, lying in wait. He doubted it, though, just by his gut, which he had come to trust as much as his eyes and ears over the years. If Shaw had a sixth sense, it was housed somewhere between his ribs and waist.

Cobb was just more than a yard behind the senior lawman, his shotgun trained at the torn screen. He slowed to a stop as Shaw came up to the wall of the screened in porch. He kept one eye shut tight as he sighted down the barrel of the shotgun, focusing in on a spot just over Shaw's left shoulder. He held his breath, watching as Shaw used the barrel of his gun to push open the flap of shredded screen. Cobb wasn't certain, but he thought he saw a wobble in Shaw as the sheriff got the first look inside. Slowly, Shaw pulled the shotgun barrel out of the hole, and let it point towards the ground, hanging loosely in his left hand. Cobb opened both eyes, and slowly came forward.

"Boss?" Cobb asked softly.

"We're clear," came a raspy reply. Shaw sounded like he had a throat full of phlegm and needed to cough. As Cobb lowered his gun, he realized that it wasn't phlegm clogging Shaw's throat. It was bile.

It took Cobb a long moment to identify the body they were looking at. What made it difficult was the degree of mutilation, and the sheer volume of scattered body parts. When Cobb saw the mop of bushy hair atop what looked like a shattered half a canteloupe, he determined it to belong to Walter. Whatever had happened to Shaw's brother-in-law hadn't left much of Walter intact. Ewell had been right with his tormented, one word description. Pieces. All Cobb and Shaw could see were pieces.

"Russ, run back to the Ranger and grab us some rubber bands," directed Shaw.

Cobb hesitated. "Why don't we call this in and let State take it," he suggested, trying to keep Shaw from investigating any further. He would volunteer to do the interior sweep, to make sure there were, or were not, any survivors.

"You work law in a small community, you know the rules, Russ," Shaw said coldly, reminding the deputy of the truth they both knew all too well. "Sooner or later you're gonna investigate your own...one way or the other."

"I'll be right back," Cobb agreed, trotting around the driveway side of the building. When he returned, he handed Shaw two thick, matching rubber bands. Shaw noted that Cobb had already placed two different width bands on the fronts of his shoes. If the state investigators and the crime techs found foreign footprints within the Grove house, they would be able to rule out Shaw or Cobb as the source.

"You want me to lead?" Cobb asked, even though he already knew what the answer would be. Shaw was pulling on a pair of latex gloves. Cobb, who had almost forgotten his own, snapped a pair on.

Shaw used his keys to pry back the loose screen door and swing it open, even though he doubted that there were any latent fingerprints on the door handle to preserve. Connors Glen was one of the last places he'd imagined that he'd need to use techniques designed to preserve the integrity of a crime scene—particularly a murder scene—but the state paid for the training every other year to keep local law enforcement up to date. What he'd thought of as frivolous for his officers and himself to a degree, was now proving to be valuable. Or so he hoped.

Walter Bennings' upper body was devoid of both arms, and his head was in a dozen pieces, of which two of the largest rested about eight feet from one another on the floor. Blood was everywhere. It was on all of the porch furniture. Spray had showered the screen of a television and the rolling cart it rested on, and by the door leading inside, into the kitchen, there was a huge pool of crimson. It was already congealing, attracting some straggling, early fall insects. Shaw stepped carefully over two large pools and stood poised to enter the kitchen.

Cobb crouched down and tried to make heads or tails of a shape he had spotted beneath a table. At first it looked like a wet, rolled up blanket. He eventually made out what looked like a seam, and finally recognized what it was that he had been looking at. It was the ass of Walter's pants. As Cobb came around the table, he found himself looking into Walter's pelvis. A strand of ropy intestine stretched out across the wooden floor was all that had been left attached to a ragged chunk of tissue that had been part of Walter's abdomen. Cobb felt his eyes watering; he had never seen anything like this, not even in a cop's worst nightmare.

"Oh God," sighed Shaw. Cobb rose to his feet and saw the sheriff's back as his boss blocked out the doorway into the kitchen. Shaw's shoulders were slumped, and the big man was leaning up against the bloody door frame. Cobb stepped around the table and tiptoed around a number of patches of torn flesh and blood spatter.

"Come on, boss, let's back out and get a breath. We're not catching any bad guys here, you and me both know it. I'll finish the sweep, and we'll let the guys from State—" Shaw took a step forward, vacating the doorway. What met Cobb's eyes was absolute carnage—nothing less. If it were possible, what had been done to Shaw's sister Vickie was more horrifying than the fate that had befallen her husband.

Cobb eyed the spot on the kitchen tile where Shaw was staring, transfixed. The top of Vickie's head rested on the floor, torn off just beneath her eyes. They were both intact, and open, lifeless but frozen wide in terror at what she had faced just before she had been killed. Cobb turned away, unable to look into those eyes any longer.

The whole kitchen was awash in dripping streaks of plasma. It looked like somebody had turned a garden hose on inside and sprayed the whole room indiscriminately. However, instead of water, what had flowed here was sinister and crimson. Spray and splatter marked every wall and cabinet. There was blood on the blades of the ceiling fan, which was still spinning on low above them. The floor was soaked, as were the countertops. Just to the right of the sink, one of Vickie's arms rested, the bones in her forearm both exposed through gaping holes where her flesh and muscle had once attached it to her body. It looked like some of her fingers were missing, but it was hard to tell, considering how badly her hand had been mangled. Reviewing the carnage, Cobb reluctantly proffered an opinion.

"You don't think this could be a bear, do you?" Shaw shook his head.

"I don't think so. I don't see any traces of anything that would make me think bear. I think if this was a bear, the whole place would be destroyed, not just...them."

Shaw's radio sounded on his hip. He lowered the volume and asked Gail where she was.

"About a mile out," she responded. "Station's covered, Ed's waiting on the word from you. What should I tell him?"

"Have Ed radio state," Shaw said reluctantly. "Tell them we have at least a double homicide. Tell them to bring the techs, and to expect a bad scene." There was a long moment of silence as Gail processed the news.

"Ten-four, Sheriff... I'm terribly sorry."

"Thanks, Gail. Me and Russell have the second floor to sweep. When you arrive, set up a tape perimeter. Mark it twenty feet around the whole building. Wait by the front of the house, we'll meet up out there."

"Ten-four," confirmed Gail, her voice wavering. Shaw and Cobb both knew that Gail signed off before she lost it over the police band. Shaw hoped she pulled over to relay the information to deputy Shulusky and composed herself before they met up. Shaw didn't mind the fact that she was upset—he just didn't want to see her when they came out of the house and lose it himself.

Shaw led the way into the hall. At the mouth of it, both men were forced to step over one of Vickie's feet. It had been severed just above the ankle, and was still in a furry, bunny slipper, the white fur soaked with blood. A few feet deeper into the hallway, both men could make out a large object on the floor. Shaw couldn't be certain what it was, but didn't want to take any chances.

"Roscoe?" he called softly, raising the shotgun to sight the object in. He gestured to Cobb to hit the light switch, which Cobb flipped with the muzzle of his gun.

The hallway light blazed brightly for a moment, then flickered. It bathed the hallway in enough light for Shaw to see that it was not a wounded or dead Roscoe laying at the end of the hallway, but his sister's ribcage. The hallway walls were speckled with blood, and the light bulb was stained with it as well. Enough so that within seconds, it had burned itself out.

Shaw walked past the huge portion of his sister's corpse without a second look. Cobb wished he had done the same. As he stepped gingerly past it, he looked down and saw half of Vickie's right breast, still attached to the bony frame. Her bathrobe sprawled out beneath, a small portion of shoulder and bone still holding the arm of the robe around it. Cobb shook his head and fell in behind Shaw, who was now face to snout with Roscoe's remains, halfway up the stairs to the second floor.

The retriever was remarkably intact, compared to his human counterparts. The damage seemed to have rained down on the mutt's head. It appeared that something had torn Roscoe's head apart at the jaws, and then ripped a gaping wound into the dog's side. Shaw was looking closely at the dog's teeth, and seemed to have found something. He motioned Cobb nearer, keeping an eye trained towards the top of the stairs.

"Get a look at this...looks like hair. Black hair."

"Maybe old Roscoe got some licks in," offered Cobb, looking at the hairs clenched in the dog's teeth. They were embedded between them like floss. Cobb didn't believe it himself, but a bear attack was becoming at least a possibility in his mind.

"I'm going to check Kyle's room, you go towards the master bedroom and see if there's anything up here that might be important." Cobb took the directions and moved towards the east side of the second floor. Shaw moved west, towards the only room on that side—his nephew's.

Shaw was surprised as he was met with the smell of fresh air upon entering the boy's bedroom. Across from him, to the right of Kyle's unmade bed, the window was fully open. On the other side of the room, the window with Kyle's air conditioner was intact. The boy's closet door was open, a pair of blue jeans hanging on the doorknob, his laundry bag—stuffed to overflowing—hanging on the other side.

"Kyle?" tried Shaw, his hope rising. There was no response. A quick glance around the room satisfied the sheriff—his nephew was not inside.

"Nothing," Cobb reported, arriving at the boy's doorway. "Whole floor looks clear."

"He's not here, Russ," Shaw said nervously, not sure whether or not it meant anything as far as his nephew's safety went. He had at least the one positive to go on, however—they had yet to find pieces of the 14-year-old in the house. Shaw could at least hold onto that. They heard Gail pull up outside.

"You go down and tell Gail what's what," said Shaw. "I want to see if there's anything here. Maybe he was staying at the MacDonald's tonight, with Boomer's kids. Have Gail run that down. I'm gonna snoop."

"Got it. The window open when you came in?"

"Yeah, first thing I saw," responded Shaw.

"Maybe old Roscoe was the last line of defense. You think maybe—?"

"I dunno, Russ, but I'm hoping. Anything's possible." Both men looked at the window, and then Cobb made his way back down the stairs to help Gail, and keep her away from the house. Shaw surveyed the room, tried to envision it as it always was, trying to intuit if there was anything he was missing.

Had Kyle been roused by Roscoe and seen the dog struggling with a bear in the house? It seemed out of the realm of the fantastic, but it was as likely a scenario as could rationally explain both the massacre and the hair in Roscoe's jaws. Could his 14-year-old nephew have dropped the twenty-odd feet to the ground and escaped? If so, why hadn't he called Shaw? Injured, maybe? In shock? Shaw sat on the edge of his nephew's bed and wondered. Right now, there were too many possibilities to consider. He didn't have enough pieces to the puzzle yet.

Pieces...

He was about to leave the room when he heard a trill of bells. On Kyle's desk, his monitor sat dark, but the CPU was still running. Shaw went to the computer and nudged the mouse. The screen returned to life. Kyle was still logged on, his AOL and an Internet window filling the screen. Kyle had just received an instant message with a hyperlink from the screen name SexxxyBa8e69. He was being invited to share hot sex talk with a college freshman who needed to sell nude pics of her and her friends to make their tuition. Shaw closed the spam window and looked at the menu. He brought up the AOL clock. Kyle had been on, according to the timer, for over ten hours. That wasn't promising. If he had been online early last night, and something had happened downstairs, it eliminated the potential for him to be safe over at the MacDonalds'. It did bolster the possibility that Cobb seemed to be liking, though. A bear attack from which Kyle had escaped, using the bedroom window. Shaw would have preferred Kyle to be sleeping at his friend's house, but even if Cobb was right, it meant Kyle had escaped what had happened downstairs.

Shaw decided to leave the computer on, in case the techs could see if Kyle had sent any messages or alerted anybody that something was happening at the house. He minimized the Internet site, but then brought it back full screen. For some reason, maybe homework, Kyle had been surfing lunarcycle.com. Shaw laughed, in spite of everything. He had half expected to find that Kyle had been surfing ESPN.com, with scoreland.com or some other adult Web site he and his friends had scammed a password to in the background. Kyle had confided to Shaw just a few months earlier that his parents were none too bright when it came to their home computers, and that the only system they had locked down from adult sites had been their own. Shaw had promised not to rat his nephew out. Of course, that had come at a cost. Shaw wanted the password, too. Lawman or not, he wasn't going to let a free password go to waste.

Shaw shut off the monitor, and listened as a wail of sirens sounded in the distance. That would be the state troopers, and the crime scene unit. Just in time, too. Shaw was ready to leap out Kyle's window to escape himself.

Cobb had already briefed Gail by the time Shaw emerged from the Grove house. She had done her best to try and compose herself, but the red circles beneath her eyes gave her away. Like Cobb, she had been the guest of many a Grove house barbecue and birthday party. The whole Connors Glen police department had. When this news spread, it was going to hit a whole community hard.

Shaw patted Gail on the shoulder and she gave him a hug in return. Sprawling out on the lawn now were four state trooper vehicles and a large, white panel truck— the county evidence technician's van. Shaw had only seen the van at the state trooper barracks in Westfield, and once at the scene of a major accident out on Route 191 a few years back. Drugs had been spotted on the passenger side floorboard of one of the devastated vehicles. So had the head of one of the passengers from the back seat. It had been quite a scene.

The trooper in charge of the investigation was a lieutenant named Lonergan. He came over, exchanged introductions with the Connors officers, and directed his team to get their system set up. Lonergan had already been filled in that the victims were members of Shaw's family. Aware that Connors Glen was a dust speck on the state map and rarely, if ever, encountered anything like what had been described as a double-homicide with savage victim mutilation on site, he tread lightly on what had gone on thus far procedurally.

"We both did a full sweep," Shaw said. "Might not have exactly gone by the book, but we did our best not to compromise the scene or any evidence. There's a lot in there, though. I think your guys have their day cut out for 'em." Lonergan noted the two men had banded their shoes and were still wearing gloves. A promising sign, if his techs were going to recover useful evidence inside.

"Anything besides the decedents that you saw inside?" asked Lonergan. Cobb shook his head. Shaw looked up from the perch he had taken on the back bumper of Tasker's cruiser.

"You got a computer tech with you?" asked Shaw. "My nephew was signed on AOL, maybe you can see if he sent anything or if there's anything he did when he was on that might help us find him."

"Yeah, one of our labbies is a backup info guru. Hey Nicole, c'mere a minute." A tall, slender blonde in her late twenties walked to where Shaw, Cobb and Lonergan were gathered. She was a member of the evidence collection team, and did double-duty on the team's computer system.

"Sheriff, this is Officer Vila, she knows her stuff on any type of box. You say the computer is in your nephew's room?"

Shaw nodded. "Top of the stairs, to the left. I left everything as is, I think he's still signed on. We haven't found him yet. It looks like he was at home when things happened last night, and might have had a chance to get out of the house." Vila was jotting down info on a small notepad.

"How's the organization for a search coming?" Lonergan asked.

"We've got assistance coming up from the Somerset fire department and some of their locals, and we're organizing our lost child search system at the station. We expect to have about a hundred, maybe hundred-and-fifty searchers here within the hour. We're going to stage them on the other side of the field there, so they don't compromise anything in the immediate perimeter," offered Gail, who had been working the radio and cell phones hard. It had been two years since they had to perform a missing child search. The last time it had been in the woods, as well. Luckily, they had been successful with Blair Bright's three-year-old daughter. Gail was already praying for a similar result here.

Good, the sooner we can start spreading bodies into the woods, the better shot we have if he's in there. I'm going to have some of our team start a preliminary search to see if they can't pick up on anything. We have a dog team coming in from county, should be here in about half an hour, forty minutes, too. We've got a lot of resources, Scott. We're gonna find him." Shaw nodded his appreciation. Lonergan had a tech run through the layout of the Grove house with Shaw, and sent Vila and two evidence techs in to begin their work.

Shaw was again left alone with Cobb and Tasker. A brief, uncomfortable silence was broken when the radio on Gail's hip crackled to life.

"Tasker, go ahead."

"Gail, Will just got done over at the MacDonalds'. He says Boomer's boy didn't see Kyle at all yesterday, even after school. He says that Boomer wasn't one hundred percent sure, but he thinks that Chris told him Kyle was grounded but he didn't know why."

The voice coming across on the radio was Lucille's. A part-time deputy's assistant, she technically wasn't an actual officer, but worked at the station as a sort of dispatcher and secretary. She was also a coordination genius. It was Lucille who ran the missing child search program. Every year, she ran a full-scale practice drill and she made sure her volunteers knew exactly what they were doing. Having Lucille whipping that program into action now offered Shaw some small measure of relief. Lonergan's guarantee came back to him. "We'll find him," Lonergan had said with confidence. Shaw wondered. Even if Lonergan made good, Shaw was of shaky faith that they would find his nephew intact.

Seven hours had passed. Shaw stood, staring helplessly out into the woods where the search teams had disappeared from his sight long hours before. He wanted desperately to be leading one of those teams, but reluctantly he accepted the fact that he could not. Lonergan hadn't yet done anything to squeeze Shaw out of a role in the nuts and bolts of the investigation, but, then again, Shaw was the most valuable source of inside information they had, and questions had been coming from the techs through Lonergan sporadically all day. Gail had been sent back to the station to relieve Lucille, and Cobb had been drafted to assist some of the troopers as they read the area maps. An avid hunter, Cobb had grown up in these woods, and so was invaluable in assisting the non-locals on the terrain they would be facing the further into the woods they explored.

Shaw felt the odd man out, unable to engage in the investigation the way he wanted to. He had been keeping his frustration in check thus far, but as he noted a bit of commotion and activity going on by the back of the crime tech's evidence van, he made the conscious decision to nose in.

Vila was going over something with Lonergan. She held a few sheets of paper in one hand and the two of them seemed to be trying to make sense of whatever it was that she had brought to the lieutenant's attention. As Shaw neared, he began overhearing snippets of their conversation.

"...kill, something?" Lonergan suggested.

"Could be, but that would still leave what you saw inside, and I don't think any 14—"

"How goes it?" Shaw interjected, making his presence known. He knew the intrusion would likely irk Lonergan, but he was tired of standing on the sidelines.

"Nicole found something in your nephew's computer calendar," Lonergan stated. Vila was holding out a sheet to Shaw. The day before marked the only entry for the month. The initials "KC" and a small exclamation point with little lines emanating from it looked back at him.

"KC?" he asked.

"Exactly," responded Vila. The icon denotes an event or appointment flagged as important. That leaves us with KC, and whether or not it means anything relevant to what happened to your sister and brother-in-law. I couldn't find anything in Kyle's address book that matches KC," Vila concluded. Shaw tried to think of anybody his nephew might have known with the initials. He knew all of Kyle's friends, especially in a town this small. Nobody came to mind.

"Officer Vila is going through your nephew's history files for the past few days," Lonergan informed Shaw. Maybe there's something you can help her out with if she has any questions." *If...* Shaw got the hint. Hang around and wait to be useful, but only if asked. He took the copy of the printout and headed back towards the Ranger. He'd been sitting in the cab monitoring the scanner for most of the uneventful past few hours. Maybe he could crack the mystery of what KC was if he gave it some time. He could also stay in touch with Cobb and the station without getting in the way.

There was chatter on and off on the scanner, but nothing of substance. Shaw sat in the cab of the Ranger and let his head rest against the top of the seat. A breeze blew through the open windows, making it comfortable to sit and think, until the occasional change in wind direction blew a whiff of death and decomposition to his nose. The mystery of KC rattled back and forth in his head like dice with missing dots. He couldn't associate the initials with anything. He checked his dashboard clock, noted the time. It was nearly three-thirty, when Kyle would usually be returning home from school. Shaw closed his lids and held them shut tight. If Kyle had managed to escape, why hadn't he tried to contact the station? Something had to have happened to keep the boy from contacting Shaw, of that the sheriff was certain. Thus far, though, there was absolutely no evidence of kidnaping. The techs had spent a long time working over the window in Kyle's room. There were no latents on the outside of the window, nor on the sill, making the possibility of a ladder-climbing intruder highly unlikely. By the same token, the techs had recovered prints all over the interior of the window as well as the sill. They were fairly small prints, and the consensus among the techs was that they were likely Kyle's prints. They had found the same size prints on objects buried deep within the boy's closet, on shafts of his hockey sticks, on a water bottle and several other objects. Until they were run, they could not be sure, but at the moment, they were what they called "lawman sure." The odds of the prints belonging to anybody other than Kyle were remote. They didn't totally rule out kidnap, but put that in with the remotest of possible explanations.

For the first time since he had snuck a doughnut out of the box he'd brought in to work that morning, Shaw felt a rumbling in his empty gut. He sighed, thinking about how on an ordinary day he would have stopped by his sister's place and grabbed a snack while Kyle got ready to do whatever he was planning to do after school, like going down to—

School. Shaw sat up in the Ranger and thought about that. Lucille had sent deputy Will Jensen over to Boomer MacDonald's to find out if Kyle had slept over there. Kyle's best friend was Boomer's son Chris. The boys had grown up together and were virtually inseparable. They played on the school basketball team, they had each taken turns breaking all the windows in Boomer's garage with hockey pucks, and they often spent the night at either Boomer's or Kyle's. They were as close as a pair of brothers. Shaw recalled Kyle once having told him that he could tell his best friend anything, when the two were talking about something Kyle hadn't been able to broach with his dad—girls. Shaw thought about what his nephew had said...he could tell Chris MacDonald anything. Shaw stuffed the key into the ignition and the Ranger roared to life.

Maybe Chris MacDonald had an idea who, or what, KC stood for.

Shaw radioed in his location to both the station and Lonergan's crew. He'd be able to be reached in the event that they found anything, or needed to get any information from him. He pulled into Boomer's driveway at just past 3:40. Chris had probably been home for at least half an hour. Shaw knew it likely that he had already heard the bad news. When he got to the side door, Nan was already there, waiting for him.

"Scott, I am so sorry. I don't know what to say," Nan said, wrapping her arms around the sheriff. "I can't believe it's possible."

"I know," agreed Shaw. "Certainly not here."

"Deputy Will was here right as Chris was leaving for school. He was gone before I could stop him. By the time Will told me what had happened, I decided to wait until he got back home to tell him. He's been stomping around in his room ever since because I wouldn't let him go help search."

"I'll talk to him. It's 18 and over anyway, and we have a lot of people out there already. Lot of people from State, too."

"Good, good, the more the better. What can I do? Do you need me to help out with anything?"

"Actually, I just want to talk to Chris about a few things. You know those two, they're practically the same kid. If I could just talk to him for a few minutes, see if Kyle said anything the last few days, see if there's been anything he was worried about, anything weird..."

"Of course," agreed Nan, pointing towards the steps. "You want me to call him down or you want to talk upstairs? He's still going to be real sore at me." Shaw gave Nan a small smile.

"I'll go upstairs. I can understand how he feels, I'm kinda in the same boat. Don't worry, I'll get you off the hook."

Shaw went up the stairs and saw only one door shut. Hearing shuffling from behind it, he gave a knock.

"What?" came an angry, defiant voice. Nan was right. Chris was about as polite a kid as they came.

"Chris? It's Sheriff Shaw...Can I come in?" The door opened almost instantaneously.

"Sorry, Sheriff. Did Mom change her mind? Can I come down and help?" There was so much hope in Chris' voice Shaw felt guilty that he could not grant the boy his wish. Chris' face was still red. He had been crying.

"Wish I could, Chris, but for right now you and me are both on the outside looking in. I wanted to ask you a few things, if that's okay, though. Maybe that'll help out."

"Sure, Sheriff, anything." Chris stepped back into his room and sat down on the edge of the bed. "You can have my chair," he offered Shaw. The room was remarkably similar to Kyle's, messy and unkempt and full of life. A Marshall Faulk poster hung on the wall—Kyle was less a football fan and had a Mario Lemieux poster on his wall. Aside from that, and the color of the paint, the rooms could have been interchangeable. Shaw took a seat in the metal folding chair that sat in front of Chris's computer desk.

"I'm awful sorry about Aunt Vickie and Uncle Walter," Chris said softly. Shaw saw the boy's eyes getting glassy with tears. He knew Kyle considered the MacDonalds as an Aunt and Uncle, too, though no blood relation existed.

"So am I, kiddo. It's been a lousy day all around. They won't let me search, either, so don't give your Mom too rough a time, okay?"

"I understand," the boy acknowledged.

"Let me ask you something, Chris, maybe you can help me out. You think Kyle might have been grounded last night?"

"I know he was. He got in trouble two weeks ago," Chris responded.

"Two weeks?" Shaw asked, surprised. "He got grounded for two weeks?"

"Not two weeks straight, just two Wednesdays," Chris explained, although his answer seemed to be all the more puzzling. Who ever heard of a kid being grounded on Wednesday nights?

"Wednesday night grounding? Do you know why?" Chris fidgeted uncomfortably. Shaw felt he was on to something. "Chris, whatever you tell me stays between the two of us. You know that, right? I need to know if it might in any way help me find Kyle. Anything you tell me, even if it's bad? Only me. I'm the only one who'll know. Not Kyle, not your parents, nobody."

"Okay..." Chris sighed. "Kyle got caught lying two weeks ago about going to the movies instead of going to Bingo with me. I was kinda covering for him, because I go work it with my dad. Nobody ever asks about it, so we figured nobody would find out, but Aunt Vickie did. I think she found the ticket stub in his pants or something, so he got grounded for the next two Wednesdays."

"He lied about going to the movies? Why?"

"Remember a few weeks ago that movie *The Garbage Man* was playing? It was rated R, and Aunt Vickie and my Mom wouldn't let us go."

"If it was rated R how was he going to get in?"

"Billy Kaser's brother, Bobby, works there on Wednesday nights. He doesn't care who he lets in, if there's nobody gonna catch him. " Shaw wanted to laugh at the ingenuity of the two 14-year-olds. This was a secret worth keeping to them— sneaking in to the movies."

"So he went alone?" Shaw continued. He saw a look cross Chris' face and knew he was going down the right road. Now Chris was really uncomfortable.

"Uh, I don't know," the boy lied. This was probably a factor which had led to Kyle getting busted. Neither boy was too good a liar.

"You don't know? Chris, c'mon..."

"Honest Sheriff, I don't know. It's just..."

"Just?"

"Okay, I think—I'm not sure, but I think he might've had, you know, a date." Chris confided. Shaw sat back. Suddenly, a lot had been explained. He went back again to the conversation he'd had with his nephew almost a month ago. That would have been two Wednesday cycles back. The time frame fit. If Kyle had pulled the stunt and gone to the movies with a girl, then had gotten caught two weeks earlier, being grounded the previous evening would have been a pretty big blow. The town theater changed titles every other Wednesday. Yesterday, a new film would have been scheduled to open. Shaw found himself absent-mindedly looking over Chris' desk. On it he saw a small silver frame with a picture of the two best friends in it. It had been taken the winter before, at the county ice hockey tournament. Both boys were in a hockey stance, leaning over their sticks and gritting their teeth menacingly. Then Shaw noticed something else that clicked. Their jerseys. The logo was a shield with a fasces in the center, with and anchor and a short sword crossed behind it. It contained two letters that stood out clear as day. KC—the Knights of Columbus. Boomer was the Knights of Columbus president...the K of C hall was where they held Bingo night every Wednesday. Shaw now had a good idea of what Kyle's original plan had been. Was it possible that Kyle had tried pulling a Houdini behind his parents' back? Shaw had serious doubts about Kyle using a second floor window without a ladder to pull off the stunt, especially if his parents had both been awake. Then again, he had once been a horny 14-year-old, too. How far would he have gone to meet a girl he was sweet on?

"Something wrong, sheriff?" Chris asked.

"Actually, no. In fact, you cleared up a lot. Do you know who it was that Kyle was sneaking out with?"

"No. Kyle only asked me to cover that night with the Bingo thing. I think it might have been Patty Ann Brewer, though, maybe that's why he didn't tell me for sure."

"Why wouldn't he?"

"Well, we used to make fun of her, cause she had buck teeth, you know? But she got braces, and she's, you know, starting to get..." Chris put his hands in front of his chest. Shaw smiled.

"I got you," Shaw replied, understanding all too well.

"It might not have been her, Sheriff, I really don't know. I just figured since we always used to make fun that maybe he wanted to keep it a secret."

"Yeah," Shaw agreed. "I can understand. Did Kyle e-mail you or send you any instant messages last night?"

"No e-mail," Chris replied. "And I wasn't around to get any IMs. I was at Bingo with my dad."

"Oh, right." Shaw stood up. "Chris, thanks, you really helped, trust me. And like I said, nothing goes any further than this room, okay?"

Chris shook his head. "It doesn't matter, Sheriff, not if it helps. Just find him, okay?"

Shaw took one last look down at the two boys pictured in the frame. He wished he could give the hurting teen a guarantee. He was given a reprieve when the radio on his hip sounded.

"Shaw here," he said anxiously. The voice that came back was Lonergan's. It was not expected.

"Sheriff, you still out at the MacDonalds' place?"

"Yeah, just finishing up. What've you got?"

"Nothing on your nephew, I'm afraid, but the techs have turned up some things. Are you headed back this way?"

"I'll be there in ten minutes, tops," Shaw informed the Lieutenant.

Shaw had made some discoveries. He hoped Lonergan's team had done the same.

Cobb was nowhere to be found when Shaw returned to the perimeter at the Grove house. In a temporary tent that had been erected to act as the base of operations for the search teams, about a dozen locals were going over maps and drinking bottled water. Shaw saw Lucille poring over a map with a pair of local shopkeepers, marking something down with one of her handy red pencils. Lucille was truly old school. Shaw would have it no other way. Rather than try to catch her attention, he ducked behind a string of vehicles, and made his way over to a new arrival, a state evidence processing mobile trailer. It looked like a government issue Winnebago. Standing by a side entry door, was Lonergan, leaning out to wave him over. Shaw hopped up into the trailer and waited for Lonergan to bring him up to speed.

"You had any trouble with rogue animals recently? In town or otherwise?"

"Rogue animals? Like what, an escaped circus elephant?"

"No, sir," one of the techs, seated at a foldaway table piped in. "Anything predatory. Bears, coyotes, wolves?"

"Are you trying to suggest this is some kind of animal attack?" Shaw asked, dubious at the suggestion. "Is that what you guys are thinking?"

Lonergan stepped back in. "We've gathered some compelling evidence. It all looks to be pointing towards some sort of animal attack. I know it might seem unlikely—"

Shaw stopped the lieutenant in his tracks. He took a look around at the crew inside the trailer. There were two, bookish types who were sorting through some items retrieved from the house and a kid who looked barely old enough to shave. It was the baby-faced kid who had spoken just a moment earlier. Shaw crossed his arms. "Any of you ever see an animal attack that left what you saw in that house back there? Any of you? What the fuck do you think went through the place, a great white shark?" The two techs behind Lonergan did not make eye contact. Babyface paused a moment before he spoke.

"We discovered tooth marks and bite indentations on some of the remains, Sheriff. We also retrieved a significant amount of animal hair follicles from the dog we processed on the stairs. So far, the only evidence we've been able to gather leads us to believe this was an animal attack."

"Okay, whiz kid, you tell me this: what kind of animal massacres two human beings the way you saw inside, and leaves no tracks in rooms splattered in that much blood? Can any of you explain that? Anybody ever see anything like that?" Shaw's voice had risen, and he knew it. He could also see by the looks on their faces that none of them had been able to work out a plausible scenario that accounted for what Shaw had exposed—a tremendous inconsistency in the animal attack theory. Animals could potentially have caused such carnage, but they certainly couldn't clean up their tracks afterward, which was what they were asking him to consider. Lonergan answered.

"We've been going over that and we understand the point, believe me, we do. But so far, we have bite marks consistent with an animal attack on the decedents. We have a significant amount of animal hair in the jaws of the deceased canine within the residence. We can find no knife or weapon markings on the bone or tissue we've been processing. You tell me, how does it look?"

Shaw stopped to consider it. He knew what Lonergan was telling him in cop speak. They didn't believe it either, but faced with the old, if it walks like a duck, and quacks like a duck litmus test, they were being forced to consider this a duck.

"Let's say that for a second, the evidence points to an animal, or animals. What are we looking at? Grizzlies? Grizzlies that got in and out through a screen window and didn't tear anything apart but my sister and brother-in-law and who took care not to leave paw prints in the gallons of blood and gore splattered on every square inch of two large rooms? Is that what we're leaning towards?" Shaw's voice was dripping with sarcasm. One of the two as-yet quiet techies spoke for the first time.

"Not likely," he agreed. "Any grizzly would be impossible to place within the residence with the entry point and size of the porch and kitchen areas. As well, the hair we gathered isn't consistent with that of a bear, grizzly or otherwise."

"Okay, what's it consistent with?" Shaw asked. For a long moment, there was nothing but silence. Babyface took it upon himself to tap the computer screen he was facing.

"There are some canine characteristics, but with some inconsistency. We think it's more closely related to wolf," he explained.

"Wolf? Tell me kid, you think what you saw was caused by a wolf?"

The kid shook his head. "Me? No, but I'm the one paid to ID stuff like these hairs. They have a lot of characteristics that look like wolf. But personally? No, I find it hard to believe. If a wolf did what was done inside that house? Call Marlon Perkins, 'cause it's the biggest most violent motherfucking wolf I'd ever expect to see."

"So, where does that leave us?" Shaw wanted to know. Lonergan laid it out bluntly.

"Either we're looking for a very unusual wolf, or we're looking for something like a wolf. Whatever it is, though, we're looking for a big one, with one hell of a set of teeth." He slid a printout across the foldaway table towards the sheriff. Shaw looked at the profile of a huge set of jaws. It looked like a profile of Roscoe times three or four.

"That's the profile we generated based on the size of the bite radius we measured and a generic, canine comparison to the tooth placement," Babyface explained. "Those teeth aren't totally compatible, just as close as we could generate right here." Shaw held up the printout and extrapolated the size of the creature in whose mouth teeth this big could be housed. It was an image that strained the boundaries of Shaw's imagination. Shaw looked at Babyface.

"Kid, you a gambler?"

"Excuse me?" the tech responded, taken aback by Shaw's request.

"You a gamblin' man?"

"I guess..."

"You tell me. Face to face with the Governor, your job on the line, do you tell the man that what he's looking for is an animal with a set of choppers this big?" Shaw slid the sheet of paper in front of the tech. The kid looked him right in the eye.

"Yeah, I would," he decided.

"Good," said Shaw, satisfied at the tech's conviction. "As long as you believe it, that's good enough for right now." Shaw went back to Lonergan. "Can we talk outside for a minute, Lieutenant?"

"Sure thing, Sheriff. " Lonergan put down a stack of paper and followed Shaw out of the trailer. Outside, Lonergan was interested to hear what Shaw wanted to discuss out of earshot.

"You keeping those three under wraps?" Shaw asked, referring to the evidence techs inside the mobile lab.

"Yeah," Lonergan confirmed. "If any of that starts getting around..."

"We'll have people calling the Enquirer and minting silver bullets. If anything those guys think they've got gets out to anybody—" Shaw warned.

"I know, believe me. When Stephen—your gamblin' man—told me what he thought he had, I told him to start over again. But what he's got on this so far matches up on paper, which puts us between the rock and the harder rock if you know what I mean."

"What do you think? You think we have something like that printout running around eating people?"

"I don't know what the hell you have out here, but we both saw what was left inside. You think this was done by a human perp? That's as out of the ball park as what Stephen's got."

Shaw nodded. "You know, the first thing I thought when I looked inside, I mean really got a good look, was a chainsaw. I didn't think anything else could have caused all that. But the whiz kid already knows there wasn't any sort of blade or weapon used...All he's got is teeth and hair. I don't want to believe that this was an animal but if that's the way it goes, okay. But if we're going to start looking for werewolves and the bogeyman up in those woods this thing is going to turn into a fucking sideshow."

"You let me worry about keeping a lid on that information," Lonergan reassured him. "I'm with you. Word gets out the media will be here, along with a thousand wackos who want to mount the head on their wall running through the woods with hand cannons and god knows what else. We'll keep this one in the vest pocket. You find anything out at the MacDonalds'?"

"Yeah. KC stands for Knights of Columbus," Shaw told Lonergan, whose brow furrowed.

"Little young for the K of C, isn't he?" Shaw chuckled, then related what Chris MacDonald had told him about Kyle's grounding and clandestine date. Lonergan digested the information.

"I doubt that Kyle could have used that window for that type of thing," he mused. "But do you have a line on this kid who works at the theater? If we can run him down, we might be able to see if Kyle made it to the movies last night."

"Already got one of mine on it. When he finds the Kaser boy we'll know something. This isn't the kind of town where you don't remember who was at the movies last night," Shaw added.

"Good. I already sent every free man I had up to join with the search parties. They're all carrying a little extra firepower. They just think it's precautionary. Mostly shotguns. I think that if—" Lonergan was cut off in mid-sentence when his radio went off. He pulled it off his hip and identified himself.

"We've got something here in the woods, sir. About a mile and a half north, about an eighth of a mile west, just shy of the Reed River Creek. "

"Is it related to the Bennings boy?"

"No sir, but we do have remains. Human remains that don't match the description of the missing boy. We're taping the area off right now."

"Any identification with the body?"

"Negative thus far, sir. But we're still looking, so it's possible."

"Did you check for a wallet?" Lonergan asked.

"Negative, sir, that's been difficult. Due to the circumstances," came the response.

"Too difficult to check for a wallet?" Lonergan asked.

"Too difficult to find the lower half of the remains, sir. The decedent has been...torn in half, lieutenant."

Lonergan looked at Shaw. "C'mon. Let's get that mountain boy Cobb and get a look at what they've got in there." Shaw watched Lonergan turn and head towards his vehicle.

"Where are you going?"

Lonergan turned back, keys in hand as he opened the trunk. He came back into view with a shotgun and box of fresh shells.

"I'm not going up there without some extra firepower, too," he remarked. "You want one of these?"

"Got my own," Shaw said, pausing at the Ranger to retrieve it once again. He double checked the load in the barrels and pocketed extra ammo. He thought about the printout that Stephen had produced as his eyes met Lonergan's.

"Ready?" the trooper asked.

"For anything." Shaw sighed, questioning in his head if that was even close to the truth.

Even with Cobb leading the way to the sector where the remains had been discovered, it was a slow, forty-five-minute hike into the teeth of the woods before the deputy, Shaw and Lonergan got to the site. Yellow crime scene tape had been looped around a hodge-podge of trees on the uneven terrain. They had made the best possible effort to establish a grid in which the techs would be able to work and map out all the evidence they might recover. By the time Cobb had led the trio to the site of the remains, the pair of troopers who had discovered the body had located its legs. They had not been found together. The right leg and foot necessitated the taping of a second perimeter, which one of the troopers was just completing.

"Still no ID?" Lonergan questioned. One of the troopers shook his head in the negative.

"No wallet yet, sir, just the parts we've found so far. We're still missing the head, some ribs, and the left foot."

"Well, keep looking, maybe the sheriff has a missing person who fits—"

"No need to check," said Cobb. "Sheriff, look at the belt buckle and the jacket. That's Timmy Sheehan."

"Yeah, I'd say it's him, too. How long ago did he take off? About a month?"

"Yeah," confirmed Cobb. To Lonergan, he added, "Kid was a local punk. Lot of people thought he skipped town about a month ago when he and his car didn't show up home one night. He'd been telling his friends for a while about wanting to blow town as soon as he was old enough, so we looked into it. He'd pulled the last ninety bucks out of his bank account three days before he didn't come home. His parents expected that he had just headed off for someplace else. We know he has some family in West Virginia. Checked up on it a week later. Hadn't heard from them. I guess he never made it as far as we thought."

"Hey!" came the voice of the second trooper. He was about ten yards away, kneeling by a large boulder. "Got a skull over here. Man, you gotta get a look at this..." The three officers and first trooper moved nearer to investigate. Sure enough, resting against the base of a boulder was Timmy Sheehan's skull. What was left of it. The facial structure remained intact, but the top of the head had been torn out right in the center. Part of the scalp which hadn't been torn away was still attached above where one ear would have been. The missing portion looked like it had been ripped free in one, huge bite. Lonergan glanced at Shaw. Both of the state troopers and Cobb were staring at the excised cavity in the skull. The tooth marks were obvious, even to the naked eye. Something very large had bitten away the top of Timmy Sheehan's head, and to the naturalist and hunter Cobb, it had almost certainly been accomplished in one bite. Lonergan's radio squawked.

"Lonergan, what's up?"

"It's Vila, Lieutenant. We finished running the history files on Kyle's computer. He sent no e-mails, and no instant messages. He signed on just before seven p.m., which helps us a little with time of death on the two victims. Other than that, there wasn't much else we found."

"About that other thing I asked you, anything on that?"

"Yes. The boy's teacher said there was no assignment dealing with the subject matter in question. As for the Internet history, the first time we noted cookies related to this type of search came four weeks ago. For the past two nights, the only sites accessed have all been relevant to this same subject matter." Lonergan listened carefully, looking to Shaw to gauge his reaction. Cobb knew there was something going on there that he was missing, but he kept his mouth shut for the time being. When he had a moment alone with Shaw he'd broach the topic.

"Thanks Nicole, that's a big help. Make me a printout of all those web sites, and lets start seeing what we might have there."

"Already started. I'll have it ready for you by six, a preliminary sooner if you need it."

"Six should be fine," Lonergan confirmed, looking into the sky. The sun was dipping towards the horizon. Soon, it would be dark. This deep in the woods, flashlights would be as useless as candles. He would have to give the order to suspend the search until daybreak shortly, in order to get the search teams back out by darkfall. Knowing what he and Shaw did about the potential threat in the woods, Lonergan didn't dare allow the fading light to become a danger to additional people. Before he gave the directive, he would assess it with Shaw. He did not expect any resistance, but under the circumstances, it was a gesture he'd rather extend to the devastated fellow lawman.

Shaw had stalked downwind about ten feet, leaving Lonergan to his radio and Cobb and the two troopers to examine the damaged skull. Shaw had a lump in his throat that was threatening to constrict his breathing. What he had heard of Vila's update to Lonergan meant that there had been a change in theory. Now, Kyle might not just appear to be a missing escapee of the massacre at the Grove house. Now, with all the wacky theories that were brewing, Shaw knew that Lonergan had another to consider—Kyle as being somehow responsible for the killings. Shaw recalled the Web site he had seen on Kyle's computer hours earlier. For the second time in approximately a month, Kyle had spent a night researching the lunar cycle. He had been grounded by his parents, who were now dead. There were no extraneous footprints or animal tracks that had yet been discovered at the house. Shaw also knew something that Lonergan didn't, but would likely discover soon—Kyle despised the older boy, Sheehan. Sheehan had picked on Kyle on a few occasions, and last year Sheehan had spent a few hours in the Hilton after the teenager had pelted Roscoe and Kyle with eggs and squirted them with a bleach-filled water pistol. Soon enough, that would come to light. Shaw knew Cobb wouldn't mention it, but once it came out, it would be another in the tally of items that would cast Kyle under suspicion.

Lonergan brought the issue of waning daylight to Shaw's attention.

"Sheriff, I'm going to suspend the search for the night. Tomorrow morning we'll reassess and, if need be, we'll see if we can get some choppers in the sky with some illumination capability. I don't think that anything more can be accomplished tonight."

"I understand," agreed Shaw. The two troopers were using thick, plastic liners and tent spikes to secure the taped off areas and remains. There would be no way to remove the remains tonight—they would have to be protected as best as they could be until techs and forensics staff could investigate in the morning. Civilian-led search teams, which fortunately had not been in this particular area of woods, would be deployed elsewhere, giving this area wide berth. Shaw doubted that by morning the discovery of Sheehan's body would remain a secret, however. These troopers were going to eat somewhere tonight, likely some place in town. There would be a lot of them, and some facts were going to leak out and be overheard. But that would be a problem that Shaw and Lonergan would face in the morning.

Tonight, under another full moon, other problems posed a more immediate threat.

Deputy Joe Bradley had finally caught up with Bobby Kaser as he arrived for work. For the better part of the day, Bradley had been seeking to talk to the teen and either confirm or deny his attendance at the theater the night before. Kaser was one of the few in town who had not heard anything about the two deaths at the Grove house, and was stunned to hear that Kyle was missing.

"No, not last night. A couple of weeks ago he asked me to sell him a ticket to some serial killer flick, and I did, but no, not last night. Don't blame him, either."

"Why's that?" Bradley asked.

"Flick is called *Yours Forever*. Chick flick about some broad in love with a doctor going off to serve in some foreign war. Boring as shit..."

"I'll tell the wife," noted Bradley. "When you sold the ticket to Kyle last time around, do you remember if he was with anybody?"

"Actually, I think he did buy two tickets. I don't remember seeing Chris with him, but I figured that's who he was sneaking in with. Why?"

"Just checking," said Bradley. "Covering all the bases."

"Well, count me in for tomorrow morning if you haven't tracked him down yet. I hope the kid turns up in one piece."

Bradley closed his notepad and thanked the teenager. Knowing what he did about what had gone on up at the Grove house, Kaser's words resounded eerily in his head.

Lonergan was seated opposite Shaw at the sheriff's desk, which had been cleared so the team could go over the map of the area and the sectors searched in the north woods thus far. They also mapped out the area where Timmy Sheehan's decomposed remains had been discovered. They could see nothing that linked the two sites aside from the presence of victims. The rugged woods terrain presented difficulties in every direction. The only thing Cobb noted was that Sheehan's body, which they had discovered close to the river, was not too deep into the woods if one was coming directly from the east. The edge of town from that border of the forest was only about a mile, even though that area of town was largely undeveloped fringe property and open field. There seemed to be no likely reason that Timmy Sheehan would be that deep in the woods, wearing his leather jacket and engineer boots. The group was wrestling with the question: what could possibly explain his presence there?

"We got the results back on those imprints at the Grove house," announced Stephen, one of the members of the team gathered at the station. He had been checking his e-mail on a sophisticated laptop he'd jacked into the station DSL connection. "It's definitely not ladder footprints. Likely it's heels that left those in the ground." Stephen was referring to two indentations that had been discovered in the soft grassy earth directly beneath Kyle's window. Stephen continued, "No ladders matching those imprints that could reach that height make for a likely match. Our pals in D.C. say the indents are consistent with a jumper, which would explain the difference we measured in depth and shape. Chances are he landed heavier on one foot than the other, and took off from there."

"Anything on the tooth marks or the hair? You get anything back on that, Stephen?" asked Lonergan.

"Nothing you want to hear," he replied.

"What's that supposed to mean?"

Stephen took a printout from a stack of papers he'd run out of the station house printer. He began to recite the information he'd received.

"According to the staff at the State University's zoology department, the hair we retrieved from the dog at the residence most closely matches—*canis lupus*. It's very close to wolf hair. Until they can do a full work-up on the actual samples, they can only go on our initial lab comps. The other info that we have is an exact match. The scrapings we took off the bones we collected? Enamel. Human enamel." The words hung in the air. Nobody reacted immediately.

"Wolfman?" Cobb finally said. "You gotta be shitting me if this is the best you guys can do."

"Hey, you a better analyst of scientific data?" Stephen challenged, waving the printouts in the air. "We go on what we find, we don't make shit up as we go along. You got a better answer, you tell me what it is." Shaw was impressed. Under fire, no matter how outrageous the information appeared, Babyface was willing to stand by it.

"Okay you two, calm down," said the sheriff sternly. "We still have an unsolved missing persons case, and a double homicide, plus another dead in the woods. The only people who know about this so far is us. Before we start going that route, we should stick with what we do know for sure, and see what fits around that. Did I remember that right, Lieutenant?"

"That's the way we teach it," Lonergan agreed. "Okay, let's say we accept the science data on its face. If there is something up there in those woods, we have, the way I see it, only two reasonable possibilities. One, is that it exists, it's out there, and its got a monthly feeding schedule, as we've confirmed by the timing of the disappearance of the Sheehan boy and what we had here last night. Now, either Kyle was fortunate, and was able to escape, or there has to be another answer."

"Like what?" asked Cobb. Lonergan hesitated. Shaw beat him to it.

"Or," Shaw explained, "it's Kyle himself."

At fifteen-minute intervals, each unit patrolling Connors Glen reported in. The three Connors Glen cruisers were being supplemented by six additional state trooper units, circling the outskirts of town, particularly the areas bordering the north woods. So far, none of the officers had reported anything out of the ordinary. All seemed quiet, like the typical Thursday night in town. Since Shaw had suggested to Virgil Benn that it might be wise to keep the theater closed for the night, it was likely that ninety-percent of the townspeople were in their homes. One trooper checking in had noted one of the unaccounted-for ten-percent.

"Unit Six reporting in. Nothing much going on between the far east end and the town dump site. Request conformation—does this town have a lover's lane on the east side? I've seen two cars parked in what looks like a seasonal field, please advise."

Cobb looked at the map, knew instantly what the trooper was referring to. It suddenly struck him, as well, that the trooper might have inadvertently stumbled upon an explanation for Timmy Sheehan's presence in the woods.

"Roger that, Unit Six, that's a pumpkin picking field where some of the kids park for some late night, uh, social events. Please take a minute and do a roust. We don't want anybody up there tonight."

"Roger that, base." Cobb shot a glance at Shaw, who nodded in agreement with the decision. Cobb tapped the map.

"That field is here, with the lake between it and the woods. If Sheehan was up by the fields and he got spooked, heading into the woods would possibly explain what he was doing in that far. He might've been running from something," Cobb theorized.

"Makes a lot of sense," agreed Lonergan. "But have you had any other kids disappear in the same time frame? Gone as runaways? I doubt this kid was up there parked all by his lonesome."

"Not necessarily. Sheehan's been known to smoke pot," Shaw tossed in. "If you wanted to light up without anybody hassling you—particularly us—it's a given that the field is a safe haven. People have been going up there to fool around for years...everybody knows that there's a sort-of agreement between the cops and the kids. They can make out; we won't shine flashlights in on 'em."

The radio crackled. It was ten minutes past ten o'clock. Nobody was due to report in yet. Unit 6, however, had reason to.

Sam Black had been a trooper for thirteen years, and felt at home behind the wheel more than anywhere else in the world. There were few who logged the miles and double-shifted with anywhere near the frequency he did. Pulling off the paved two-lane into the southernmost corner of the pumpkin field, he was super-alert. He was feeling good about the level of protection they were bringing to their small-town neighbors, as well as riding in the six car. Mark Martin, his favorite NASCAR driver, also ran the six car, and he was sitting pretty in the Winston Cup standings after a particularly good run at Loudon, less than forty points off the lead, with a whole lot of racing left. Black was stoked for his favorite wheel-man to make a run at the Winston Cup title.

Black was also happy that he'd taken Martin's advice and given those little blue pills a try. As he killed the lights and rolled up slowly, one of the two vehicles he'd stopped to roust gradually started backing out. Black, who'd been feeling like a teenager with a perpetual boner himself, felt sorry for the couples who were going to have to go elsewhere, or take cold showers later on.

Black pulled out his flashlight and deliberately slammed the door of his cruiser. He wanted to give whoever was in the parked car the chance to get as much clothing back on as possible before he had to shoo them on their way. He came up on the vehicle and turned on the beam.

The front seat was empty, so Black angled his beam towards the back, where the light bounced off a long expanse of exposed flesh that he recognized as a girl's leg, pressed against the front seats, likely by the hips of her male counterpart. The compact, 2-door vehicle made it tough to make out anything else. Black walked around to the other side of the car, and stopped in his tracks. He saw that the driver's side door was open. And not just open, but jammed at an angle into the ground, like it had been torn from one of its hinges. The driver's side glass was spiderwebbed and caved in. On the inside of the window, Black could make out a large, dark stain. It was unmistakable.

Black nudged open the door with a firm heel to the door frame, spewing gravel as the metal gouged the ground. He pulled the driver's seat forward using the seat belt, and flashed his light on the couple in the back.

There was an enormous wound in between the boy's shoulder blades. His ribcage was exposed through the gaping wound. It looked as if he had been shot through the chest from the other side, but there was no room for the kind of firepower necessary to blow a body apart like that. Black swallowed some bile as he traced up the girl's leg to her face. He got as far as where her face should have been before he turned away. The back of her head was there, and her chin, but the rest of her face and the front of her skull had been torn away. Blood, sinus cavities and grey matter were all that was left. Black stepped back from the car and realized that the second vehicle had not started. Instead, it slowly continued to roll back down an incline towards the lake, which was illuminated by the moonlight. Black slammed his flashlight into his belt loop and pulled his radio to call for back-up. If there was somebody still alive in the car that was rolling towards the water...

The call for back-up was frantic and jerky. It sounded like Sam Black—who Lonergan had identified as the trooper in Unit Six—was running as he spoke. Shaw made out the words "two victims" and put his hand out. Cobb was already tossing Shaw a shotgun. The team was on the move.

Lonergan patched through and notified his units to converge on the field fully ready to use their firearms. With what he knew about the threat that faced his men and women, he was not going to tread into action lightly. He told his units to respond to any threat with lethal force. If it came to it, he doubted they would have time to make a force decision based on a split-second assessment. Recognizing this, he took the decision out of their hands. He hoped that was enough to give them a chance, if not an advantage.

Lonergan tried to get Black to respond before the trooper engaged the described second vehicle, but he could not get his man to communicate further. Nervously, as the team inside the station prepared to go mobile, Lonergan waited. As the team concluded their weapons check and moved towards the door, Black's voice came over the radio.

"Holy shit it's big," he managed. Static followed.

Then the radio went silent.

With nobody left to run the station, and with the magnitude of the emergency, Lonergan offered up Vila to run the communications for both the troopers and the local response. Every other available man and woman, techs included, scrambled into the few remaining vehicles, one of them being Lucille's Saturn, which she had left at the station. Lucille had gotten a lift home from one of the other search party members instead of heading all the way back to the center of town. Luckily, she had left Gail her keys. Gail jumped into the car, along with Lonergan. Shaw flipped his keys to Cobb, as he pulled extra ammo from a lock box in the cab of the Ranger.

"Everybody's pretty spread out," observed Cobb. "We'll probably be there as fast as anybody who's gotta figure out where they're going."

"Good. The faster we get there, the better. I know what Lonergan is thinking and I don't like it."

"Scott, you don't really think...you know."

"I dunno, Russ. But I know where the finger looks like it's pointing and it scares the shit out of me. Lonergan's decided already—he thinks it's Kyle." Cobb sighed. Shaw continued, "I can't say as I blame him. Look at what he's got...Kyle was at the house, likely the only survivor. The evidence, hinky as it is, all points to animal attack. He's got Kyle with an angry motive against Vickie and Walt. Kyle spends the last two nights and a few nights exactly one month ago on the Web researching the lunar cycle. Lonergan doesn't know about the thing with Timmy Sheehan last Halloween, but how bad does that look that the last time anybody saw Sheehan happens to coincide with a fucking full moon..."

"You really think this is a werewolf thing, Scott? Really?"

"Let me ask you something, Russ. You still go to church every Sunday?"

"You bet."

"Okay. What would it take to prove to most people that it was the second coming? I mean, if he really came back, without flying golden chariots and angels and all that? What if he came just like the first time? Just a man with a message who preached and was peaceful and did some stuff like in the good book. What if he came and spent a while looking around first? What would it take to

convince people? Fucking David Copperfield floats and makes the Statue of Liberty disappear and does all that shit and we all look at it like it's a joke. Hey, he put one over on us...What would Christ have to do?"

"Something pretty spectacular, I believe," Cobb answered.

"So far, Russ, all I've seen is some pretty weird shit that doesn't add up. But if I don't believe it's even possible, what if it really is what it looks like? That kid isn't yanking my chain about what the computer says those hairs are. The guy with the test tubes isn't trying to get on TV by telling us that those scrapings off my sister's bones are human enamel. Do I believe there's a werewolf out there? No, not yet, not until I see it with my own two eyes. But do I not believe there's a possibility? I can't, not after all this. And there's something else, too...Last month, Kyle came over to my place, probably the weekend after the last full moon. He was all bent out of shape 'cause he couldn't talk to Walt about what was bugging him. He had been hanging out with some girl in class, I assumed at lunchtime or something, but thinking about it, it might have been one of these secret dates Chris MacDonald was telling me about. Anyway, I knew what he was getting at, that he was sweet on whoever it was. But there was something else. He'd been telling me how uncomfortable it made him, being with her when there weren't other kids around. You know, I figured it was just how to deal with a hard-on, you know? But he made it sound like something else, something more. He told me he felt like there was weight on his chest, and that all his muscles would get tight all of the sudden. I can't think about what he told me and think that he was just a kid who didn't know the anxiety of a boner and the threat of blowing a load in your pants while you were sitting on the bleachers in the middle of the school day. Now I'm wondering, was he trying to tell me something? Something besides 'Uncle Scott, I'm horny'?"

"Hey man, it looks like it looks, I'm not going to shit you about that. But I am not giving up on a big, bad wolf-bear out there in the woods, and Kyle hiding out somewhere from it. Promise." Shaw nodded. Cobb made a hard left and led the charge of arriving vehicles at Pat's Pumpkin Patch. As they pulled in at the far end of the grass lot, they could see Sam Black's cruiser, lights still on and driver's side door still hanging open. A few yards away, Shaw and Cobb recognized Greg Mills' car. Closer to the lake was what looked like the front end of a late model Ford Taurus, its back end submerged to the midway point of the rear passenger doors. More vehicles arrived and pulled to a halt, some facing the strands of barb wire fence that encircled the lot. Lonergan deployed two pairs of troopers to the opposite side of the lot to move in, while Shaw, Cobb, Tasker and two other troopers moved towards the lake. Everybody on site had a weapon trained on a vehicle. If there were still a danger here, it would be met with an awesome array of firepower.

"Two victims!" called the trooper who was examining the Mills vehicle. His partner gave an all clear signal when he had secured Black's cruiser.

Shaw came around the passenger side of the Taurus. It was Pat Price's car. Pat ran the pumpkin farm, and had likely come by to see who was fool enough to park out in the middle of nowhere given what had happened up at the Grove house. Shaw could picture it, Pat driving by, seeing Greg Mills and his girlfriend Betty trying to get in a little private hanky panky, and instead coming up on something quite different...something similar to what had happened at the Grove house.

"One vic so far," Shaw called out. Pat's body was slumped over in the driver's seat, held in place by the seat belt. She had been decapitated. One of Pat's hands still clutched the steering wheel.

Cobb confirmed the second. He was doing a sweep along the edge of the lake with his flashlight when he saw the first pool of blood dark in the damp grass. As he followed the path, he found the fallen officer. He'd been eviscerated. Cobb knelt by the body, still warm to the touch. Black's eyes were open, staring up at the full moon above. In his right hand was his Glock. Cobb knelt close, sniffing the barrel. There was no strong scent. Black had not managed to get off a shot. Facing his attacker, gun in hand, Black had had his intestines torn out and didn't have enough time to pull the trigger. Cobb looked up at Shaw.

"I'm starting to see things your way," Cobb whispered. Lonergan joined the two men and took a knee beside his fallen trooper.

"Fuck..." spat Lonergan. "He get one off?" Cobb shook his head. Lonergan stood up, radioed for Nicole to coordinate the members of the evidence team and get them to roll the van out to process the scene. Then he directed her to call out units from Johnson County to assist.

"You got a hardware store here in town, right, Sheriff?" Lonergan asked, bitterness at Black's death souring his voice.

"Yeah, what do you need?"

"Floodlights and battery packs. I don't think we're going to have any trouble finding some signs that this thing headed into those woods. Fuck waiting until morning. I'm going in after it."

"How long do you think before Johnson sends in back-up?" asked Cobb. Lonergan shook his head.

"Doesn't matter. As long as there's a moon up, if what we think is true is true, that's as long as we've got." Shaw nodded, pulled out his cell phone.

"Who you calling" asked Lonergan.

"Pete Hardwick. Hardware store's his. He'll put together what we need and we'll send a team to go get it. That way, we can get things ready here, 'cause it's shaping up to be a long night."

Pete Hardwick only had twelve fresh dry cells and lanterns at the ready, but he gladly turned every one of them over to Shaw and the trooper teams. By the time they were rigged and ready to infiltrate the woods, it was nearing midnight.

Scouting out the treeline, Cobb had a likely entry point for the creature they were now sure that they were tracking. A print in a patch of muddy earth looked to him to be close to that of a wolf. The fact that it was about five inches longer than any other wolf track he had ever seen, and that the heel looked more like a human footprint than a pawprint was not something he wanted to discuss. After quietly alerting Shaw to the print, the deputy eradicated it beneath his boot. With this advantage, he and Shaw might be able to beat any of Lonergan's trooper teams to the beast. Shaw and Cobb both knew that Lonergan's men were now on a search and destroy mission, much as Shaw would have been in the early hours after discovering his sister and brother-in-law at the Grove house. Now, though, with the possibility that Kyle was still out there, in the woods, Shaw wanted the chance to know the truth. With all the evidence painting Kyle as a half-man half-beast killing machine, he doubted that anybody but Cobb or himself would hold off to be sure of anything. If something moved out in the darkness and couldn't identify itself, it was going to find itself full of holes. Cobb took the lantern, and attached a sling to his shotgun so he could tote it on his shoulder. He drew his service gun and chambered a round. A lifelong hunter and outdoorsman, Cobb would do the tracking, leading the way with the light and handgun at the ready. Shaw would wield his shotgun and follow. He had all the faith in the world in his deputy. Cobb was the one with the home field advantage. These were his woods, if there was something to be found within them, Cobb was the one who'd find it. Shaw was just holding onto hope that when Cobb tracked down the creature, Kyle would be somewhere else.

Twenty feet into the woods, the moonlight was no longer a factor. Occasionally, through a break in the treeline, some diluted light would filter down, but for the most part, the lanterns cut small, ten foot slices into the darkness. Shaw nudged Cobb and whispered to the deputy, "What if that thing goes out?"

"It's gonna get real dark," Cobb retorted, offering up a little black humor as he strained to try and find additional tracks.

"I'm serious," hissed Shaw. "Can you get us the fuck out of here if that thing dies?"

"No sweat," assured Cobb. He didn't let Shaw see him do it, but he used his elbow to make sure he had his mag light on his belt. The outline of the light offered him some comfort. If the dry cell did kick out, he knew enough to guide the two men back in the direction of the pumpkin field. Still, it had been a long time since he'd used stars and the moon to find his way anywhere, and none of the merit badges he'd earned as a Boy Scout were very current. He was much more wary about what the darkness might hold in store for them. If the lights did go out, the advantage shifted from hunter to hunted. That was, if the hunters, as they saw themselves, had an advantage at all.

click-click-click...click-click-click

Shaw pulled the radio off his hip. Somewhere, one of the teams had discovered something. The fact that it was not the team of Shaw and Cobb chilled him.

Shaw put his hand on Cobb's shoulder. They were all now operating on the same frequency, with the volume turned down to barely audible levels, in the hopes of offering them some protection. Cobb, who knew wildlife well, knew it was an exercise in futility, but he went along with it. Anything short of dead silence in a tree stand with deer scent or some other animal musk to mask your own scent was going to announce your presence to anything prowling the woods long before you would hear an approaching animal. He dropped into a crouch, and pulled Shaw down to a knee so he could listen. While they waited, Cobb turned out the lantern.

Ignoring his escalating fear that the lantern would not re-light, Shaw pressed the button on the radio. Only he and Lonergan could give the go-ahead to speak.

"Shaw here, report," he directed in a hoarse whisper.

"This is Lou, Sheriff, team two. We are about fifty feet east of Reed River

Creek. We have a baseball cap here, but no signs of any other clothing."

Shaw clenched his eyes tight. "Roger that, team two. Is the hat a Pittsburgh Penguins cap?"

"Affirmative, Sheriff. There's also a bloodstain on the bill. It's not very big, though," Lou detailed, trying to put the best spin on it possible.

"Keep your eyes open," Shaw said. "Over."

So now it had been confirmed. Kyle's hat, this deep into the woods, meant he had been out here for some reason. Cobb pulled Shaw's ear close to his mouth.

"That's a fuck of a long way from the Grove house, Scott. That hat alone don't mean shit...just as easy for the wind to put it out that far."

"Maybe," Shaw replied, "but not likely. I think he was out here, Russ. I'm starting to get the sense that he's still out here."

"If that's the case," Cobb whispered, "then let's be the ones to find him first." Cobb re-lit the lantern, and could feel the hot breath of Shaw's sigh of relief on his shoulder as he did so. The two men were standing up again when a loud, high-pitched screech cut through the silence.

"What the fuck was that?" Shaw asked.

"Owl," ventured Cobb.

"They always sound like that?"

"Only when they're scared or on the defensive," Cobb informed him.

"Where was it?"

"I don't know...I'm a hunter, chief, not the Terminator. I think it came from that direction. We'll move that way a piece, see if maybe there's something that stirred it up."

"How long are those things good for?" asked Shaw, gesturing to the lantern with the muzzle of his double-barrel. Cobb shook his head dismissively and led the way towards where he believed the owl had sounded its cry of alarm.

He could hear them coming.

Just a few nights earlier, this wouldn't have been possible. Tonight, it was as natural as running through the trees in nearly absolute darkness with agility and reflexes he had never imagined. Cloaked in darkness and nothing else, his bare skin tingled in the cool October night. He had a raging hard-on, and every nerve ending in his body tingled, like they had never really been alive before.

The screech of the owl cut through the night like a fresh wound. The sound of alarm in the animal's cry was a warning sign, a harbinger of things to come. When he heard it, he came to a sudden stop. His ears pricked up, his nostrils widened and flared as he took in the scents carried by the night air.

I will not feed...

He repeated it over and over to himself. His jaw twitched; the pain in his teeth and gums threatened to make him cry out and give himself away. For a moment, all the muscles in his body tensed, constricting until they were as taut as stretched wire. In his back, he could feel the flexing of his ribcage where they met his spine. Sucking wind into his lungs, he repeated his mantra.

I will not feed, I will not feed...

More footsteps, the scent of more men. He could sense them approaching long before he would see their inefficient, hand-held lanterns. But there was something else in the air. The smell of cordite and oil and burnt steel.

Guns. Big guns, and lots of them.

His muscles finally relaxed. The tension was still there, lingering just beneath the surface. His hard-on slapped painfully against his abdomen, the tip damp with precoital excitement. He looked down at his hands, scratched and smeared with blood. Her blood. He could still smell her on his fingers.

I will not feed...

Voices now, and the hum of radios. They were still hundreds of yards away, but they were getting nearer each moment he waited. If he could lead them deeper, if he could lead them to the ridge, then he would have his best chance.

Closer yet. The owl he had startled had focused them, had given them a point to follow. Just overhead, a lone bat swept through the trees, looking to feed and then head back to its roost. In one fluid motion, he reached into the air and snagged the bat in mid-flight, tearing it in half before the creature knew what had struck it. Blood streaming down his hands, he tossed the twitching nightwing to the ground, and threw back his head.

Kyle's howl could be heard for miles.

"That wasn't an owl," Cobb noted, dropping all pretense of keeping silent. The sound that echoed towards him was slightly more due north than the path he had been following. Seeing the light of another team's lantern some sixty or so yards to their immediate left, Cobb altered the course he and Shaw were tracking, and started picking their way through the trees. It wasn't long before Cobb came upon another sign of night activity. The mutilated bat.

Shining his light on the dead bat gave Cobb all the information he needed to confirm they were on the right track.

"Fresh, no doubt about it," Cobb relayed to Shaw. "We're not all that far behind."

"Think it knows that?" asked Shaw.

Cobb nodded. "That's why hunting is a sport, 'cause it's so fucking tough for us. Whatever we're after, it knows we're coming."

"So it's had the advantage all along..." mused Shaw.

"I dunno about that," Cobb challenged. "I've never had anything I've been chasing shoot back at me before."

That knowledge did nothing to allay Shaw's apprehension.

The woods north of Connors Glen grew densest near Reed River Creek, which ran down from Lake Prince, some forty miles away. The woods, like most of the county, were flat where they had been developed, and surrounded by hills and small scatterings of elevation too small to be named Mount anything. North of Connors Glen, the high point was simply called The Ridge. It was also the only spot in the woods where there was a reasonable break in the dense treeline. From the apex, you could get a good look down into forest on all sides. If the woods had one vantage point, this was where it was. Against the backdrop of a star-filled night, the moon offered a good silhouette of anything upon the elevated ground. Kyle had come here for one reason. This was the place to lure his prey.

Panting, he scurried to the top of the ridge and looked to the south and west. There were pinpricks of light growing brighter in the distance. He saw seven or eight at the moment, but he heard more footfalls approaching than that. Good, he thought to himself, the more who came, the better.

Sniffing the delicate breeze, he caught another whiff of her. It made the hair on his neck stand on end, threatened to paralyze him again as he fought to control his muscles. Muscles which sought to rebel against him.

Not now, he thought to himself. *Not yet...*

But as he tried to turn his head, the tangle of muscle and sinew in his neck swelled and grew thick beneath his flesh. His scalp started to burn with the sensation that his skin was being stretched to the tearing point. His breathing labored...this time, he might not be able to fight it.

Summoning all the strength he had, he forced his legs to carry him over the high point, towards a copse of trees in which he might be able to regain control. As he came to it, his right knee locked, and he dropped to the ground.

Swallowing was impossible. The only thing that still seemed to be under his control was his sense of smell. As he inhaled through widening nostrils, what he sensed sent tremors through his pain-wracked body.

Trapped out in the open, the agony was nearly unbearable. His joints started to give. Beneath his skin, the muscles began to peel back, to shift and regroup, his body struggling to complete the change. All the while, as he lay there unable to move, the sound of footsteps grew louder.

This time, Kyle's howl was one of fear.

Shaw and Cobb were making their way up the ridge from the southeast, while two trooper teams were approaching from the opposite slope. When Shaw saw their proximity, he tapped the button on his radio and halted everybody's progress.

"Hold tight all teams," Shaw directed. "Mike, you there?"

Lonergan's voice came back to him. "Approaching with two additional teams. Advise."

"Sound from just ahead, at the top of the ridge. We have no sight line, but we've got the upper hand if we kill the lanterns. Anything comes up over that rise, we'll see it first. Advise a hold on gunfire until we have a confirmation."

There was a long pause before Lonergan responded. "Repeat on that hold fire order?"

"Let's just be certain, and aware of everybody's position. We kill the lamps we're gonna wind up Swiss cheese if we aren't careful." Shaw knew the answer was largely a dodge, but that Lonergan would accept the hold order. Two more lanterns came into view. Shaw gave the command to all but three teams to hold back. Any more than that, and they truly did run the risk of shooting each other in the darkness.

Cobb didn't like having any of the trooper teams behind them, back-up role or not. He feared that with the loss of one of their own fresh in their minds, they would be suffering with itchy trigger-fingers. He told Shaw as much.

"We should send a pair of teams to the other side," Cobb suggested. "Tell them to—"

The howl drowned Cobb out. His head whipping around like it was on a swivel, Cobb almost dropped his gun. What he saw stunned him. It was nightmare come to life.

Atop the ridge, the creature stood, defiant. Backlit by the moon, it threw back its head and cried out into the night. From each angle, every man would later seem to have seen something different. One thing would remain consistent—it was covered with dense, matted fur, it had the undeniable, tapered nose of a wolf, and it had jaws that could easily open to accommodate a human head, whole. It stood on two legs, thick with rippling sinew and muscle. Shaw took a step forward, trying to look into the creatures eyes.

The eyes, he thought. If I can just look into his eyes...

Cobb grabbed Shaw's shoulder and took aim. In the dark, on both sides, guns drew a line on the beast. Spittle dripped from its mouth as it snarled at the men who had come to destroy it. Shaw reached down, grabbed for the lantern, and took another step forward.

The beacon that illuminated the creature's face seemed to catch it off guard. It recoiled, and raised an arm to block the light from its eyes. The eyes Shaw was so desperate to look into. Shaw took one more step forward. Just then, the bullets began to fly.

The two back-up teams didn't wait for the hold order to be withdrawn. When they saw Shaw shine the light on the creature, they took it as a signal. He had lit up the animal like a Christmas tree. When the shots rang out, the light disappeared as Shaw was dragged to the ground by Cobb, fearing crossfire.

Shaw tucked his head, feeling Cobb's arm across his chest. Shaw was shaking, but it had nothing to do with the shots flying right past him.

"I couldn't tell, Russ...I didn't get a good look."

"We might find out if we get out of this alive...fucking bozos couldn't wait until they got the order? Cheezus..." grumbled Cobb.

What seemed like minutes took only fifteen seconds. It did not take trained lawmen long to discharge their weapons in a life-and-death situation. There was silence after the last round had echoed through the woods, while everybody waited for any response. Shaw rolled over, grabbed for the lantern he'd dropped, and started to crawl forward.

"Take it slow, boss," cautioned Cobb, taking a firing stance from a knee. He still had a round in the chamber and a full clip. If the shooting gallery the troopers had turned the woods into hadn't put their quarry down, he thought the Glock would have enough stopping power to finish the job.

Shaw moved about fifteen feet, sweeping the light across the crown of the ridge. Despite all the gunfire, the only damage he saw was scarred trees. He could not discern any bloodstains on the ground near the top of the ridge, which gave him pause. Could it be possible that they hadn't hit anything at all?

Another few yards and he took to his feet. Behind him, Cobb. To his left, a trooper team had reloaded and were prepared to finish what they had started. Shaw lifted the lantern, dimming the light a bit but opening up a wider arc of illumination. Before he saw it, he heard it—the breaking of twigs and the scattering of leaves. Lump in his throat, he drew his Glock.

Kyle appeared over the top of the ridge, running full tilt towards them. When Shaw saw the boy's face, he saw the look of recognition in the teen's eyes. Then he watched that recognition turn to horror.

"Uncle Scott—" was all he managed. Then shotgun blasts tore the boy apart.

"Hold fire! Hold fire!" Shaw commanded, but it was too late. Round after round discharged until, once again, every gun but Shaw's and Cobb's had been emptied. Shaw ran to the boy's body. There was not much of it left. Shaw looked over the naked boy, the teen's skin gouged with claw marks across his chest and legs. He looked into the boy's eyes, but they were already dull and lifeless. Blood was leaking out in large pools, seeping into the ground. Shaw clamped onto the boy's outstretched right hand. In the darkness, Cobb turned back the rest of the teams and Lonergan.

The only howls left to echo in the night were Shaw's.

There were no lights on in the Cumberland home, but around the back, one first floor window was slightly propped ajar. It opened silently, allowing her to sneak back inside.

She hadn't gotten caught. Her heart was beating fast, though, as she reached under the bed and took her rolled up nightie and panties from where she'd hidden them and pulled them back on. She sat on the edge of her bed, and put her head in her hands.

Why hadn't Kyle said yes? Why hadn't he agreed to be with her? Why did he pull away from her when she'd told him about the monthly and put his hands down there so he could see and feel it for himself?

Timmy Sheehan hadn't been afraid, not on the day he'd offered her a lift and tried to get her to do things to him in his car up at the pumpkin picking field. She remembered him trying to force her head into his lap while he stuck his hand under her dress and tried to push two fingers roughly inside her. He thought she had been wet with excitement, but he found out otherwise very quickly. Before he could get her out of his car, the change was upon her, and Timmy was heading for the woods, screaming like a banshee. Sheehan learned about the monthly when she caught up with him in the woods and tore off his nuts with her teeth, holding them up for him to see. He had still been alive and screaming when she ripped off first one leg, and then the other. Now his car was resting at the bottom of the lake, and pieces of him she refused to digest littered the north woods.

Why hadn't Kyle wanted to touch her like that? When she told him about the monthly she thought he would understand, thought he would want to be with her, to be like her. When she told him that she would take care of his parents he said he didn't want to see her any more, didn't want to be her friend. And when she had found him, tired and laying half frozen to death in the woods, he wanted no part of her. When she had scratched him, had revived him, when she had shown herself, he had refused to touch her, had pulled his hands away when she had pressed them to herself so she could change, and change him with her.

But he had resisted. He had refused to let the change come, had refused to feed, as she had told him he would have to. He had let her down because he did not really love her, as he had claimed. Now he was gone, torn apart by bullets without ever knowing the feeling of the hunt.

Tears streamed down her face. The freckled, fourteen year old girl looked out the window at the fading moon. Tomorrow, the monthly would be gone, and she would be alone again. As well, the next time the monthly came, she would have to venture even further into the woods to hunt and feed.

She pressed her hand against her crotch and felt her panties growing damp with blood and excitement. She wanted to make the hurt go away, but it would not. Kyle didn't love her, and now she was faced with being alone again.

Before she went to sleep, she climbed out of bed and went to her closet. She pulled out her knapsack, and took out a spiral notebook. On the back, in an ornate and frilly design, were the heart she had drawn with hers and Kyle's initials. Angrily, she tore off the back cover, and tossed it into the trash. Now, Kyle Bennings was out of her life for good.

Satisfied, Kristin Cumberland drifted off to sleep.

p0rn

"*What in the name of the Good Lord?*" Grace Ellen sighed, peering through the narrow kitchen blinds. She set down her teacup on the fading Formica countertop and split the yellowed, plastic slats apart with slender, bony fingers. Grace Ellen's kitchen looked out across a narrow, alley-like driveway, and faced a window into her next door neighbor's den or bedroom. Which one exactly, Grace Ellen wasn't sure, but whichever one it was, it housed her deadbeat neighbor's bigger-than-necessary television. Tonight, as they were on many nights, the images on the screen were unmistakable. Distasteful and disgusting—Grace Ellen didn't need to catch more than a glimpse to know exactly what it was. Nauseating.

Grace Ellen let the blind snap back into position and shook her head. *If only the Reverend was still alive*, she thought to herself. *If only. . .* but how many times had she had that same thought these past three years? How many times had something unsettled her since he had passed away and she found herself going back, trying to envision how different things might have been? *If only...*if only they had stayed in Pennsylvania, she fantasized, if only the Reverend had taken better care of himself, if only that unstable farm boy hadn't made those filthy, unsubstantiated accusations. . . Why was it that always the innocent among His flock met with such burdens? Made to suffer without justification? Why was it His will that she and the Reverend be forced to move to this small, cracker box house? And why had the Council of Elder Ministers all felt so strongly that California was the best place for them? She sometimes would lie awake at night, wondering if that was when the Reverend had begun to grow ill. Up until then, she'd always known the

Reverend to be a fighter, a man of principle. But when those lies began to spread about him everything started to change. He'd said that it was untrue, all of it, and of course she knew that to be the case. Yet when the elder ministers had recommended the reassignment, in order to keep the church from having to endure a long and costly legal battle, he'd acquiesced. They had moved less than a month later, and they had been in California less than a year before the Reverend's health problems began. Grace Ellen couldn't help but believe there was a link there.

And now, knowing that the Reverend would never just sit idly by when he had an opportunity to do something, to try to bring one of His fallen—like this depraved neighbor who seemed to do nothing but sit at home all the time and watch smut and pornography—around to the ways of the Lord, she questioned her own strength. What of her? Why wasn't it her place to do His good work as well?

Grace Ellen looked down into her cup of weak, lukewarm tea. Why not? Why shouldn't she do something? Why shouldn't she try to make a difference? She knew in her heart that the Reverend would have.

Still, part of her held back. She was outraged—the kind of depravity she saw whenever she was unfortunate enough to look across the drive was appalling. But, at the same time, she was Grace Ellen Howarth, the widow of the Reverend Howarth. She knew from experience that she didn't command the Reverend's respect, and she truly believed that a confrontation with her repugnant neighbor wouldn't be worth her breath. What would she say to him? How was she going to tell such a creature that he was on a narrow path to eternal darkness? Would such a person even bother to listen? Grace Ellen doubted that he would, but that didn't relieve her of her duty to try to do the right thing.

She split the blinds again and peered across the shared drive. She cringed at what was displayed on the screen. A young, blonde girl was doing something unspeakable with her mouth to an unseen partner. She may as well have been a plastic doll, as far as Grace Ellen was concerned. Naked from the waist up, she possessed firm, but unnaturally large breasts—certainly not the ones that the Good Lord had provided her. No, undoubtedly she'd taken her natural, God-given beauty and let some unscrupulous Beverly Hills surgeon do his nasty handiwork, turning her into a lurid sex object. A woman who was far less a woman, only useful as a person who would do such abominable things on film. Where else could she fit in society? The only place she had was supplying people like Grace Ellen's neighbor with dirty fodder for their sinful and desperate acts of loneliness. Grace Ellen watched the girl's pouty lips open and engulf her anonymous partner. It made her skin crawl. She made up her mind, and without any more of a plan than to somehow stop this depravity, she stepped through her back door and out into the cool, dark evening.

Once out on the back steps, Grace Ellen paused to let her eyes adjust to the darkness. There was precious little beside the moonlight to illuminate her long, narrow backyard. The porch light had burned out long ago, and she didn't see the value in spending good money to replace it. Now, with long shadows yawning across the property, she was rethinking her frugality. Undaunted by the dark tendrils stretching out towards her, she shuffled down the steps and around the side of her home.

The garbage, Grace Ellen considered. There was nothing out of the ordinary in putting out some trash. Perhaps if she got his attention by rattling her old, battered trashcans her neighbor might be embarrassed and choose something better to do with his time. To Grace, this seemed like a decent plan. It only seemed flawed when she realized that from her vantage point she could hear all the horrid sounds of ungodly sex through her neighbor's window. Grace Ellen couldn't make out what was happening on the screen, but it became evident as she rattled her trash cans to no avail that the filthy moans she heard were not coming solely from the television.

"*How disgusting*," muttered Grace Ellen. Her face registered a sour expression as she stepped back into the shadows and retreated up the porch steps. Two steps up, she could once again see into her neighbor's window. Now, she could see her neighbor, if only in part. It didn't matter. Seeing his furiously pumping right hand as it stroked his swollen flesh made her avert her eyes. She realized that simply rattling her trash bins wasn't going to be sufficient to stop his sinful conduct. Grace Ellen recoiled as the moans grew louder, the unwitting effect being that she was afforded a better view of her neighbor's abhorrent behavior, continuing on undeterred across the driveway. She was just a step from her back door when powerful, clammy hands swept up her body and clutched her around the waist and throat.

Grace Ellen struggled, but before she could open her mouth to scream she felt pressure and a burning sensation beneath her chin. A mouthful of loose but purposeful teeth tore away her larynx and the upper part of her trachea. Her vocal chords were ripped away as a crimson plume showered through her screen turning her once-cream colored curtains red. As the rough hands slammed her frail body back first against the screen door, Grace Ellen looked into the half-rotted face of her assailant.

The mangled face was gray-green and smelled of rotting chicken entrails left out in the garbage too long during a heat wave. The face only had a single, visible eye, the right one. The left one was either a victim of decay, or had collapsed into the misshapen face because of a broken cheekbone. The whole head seemed to be sinking in on itself, like an overripe jack-o-lantern. Grace Ellen could see the monster chewing up the flesh it had just excised away from her throat. She knew she was finished. She wondered if the warm feeling spreading through her chest was the signal that death was near—that the Lord was calling her home to be joined eternally with the Reverend. Or maybe it was just the flow of her own blood pouring out of her.

Losing her strength, Grace Ellen slowly began to slump towards the ground. She could feel the night air around her growing colder, and wished she had more faith that the warm feeling she was experiencing really was the Spirit laying It's hand upon her. Then the beast clutched Grace Ellen by her hair and set about trying to rend more flesh from her still-living body before she stopped breathing and was no longer of value to him. Grace Ellen's remaining strength was sapped as she wrenched her head to the side so as not to have to see her killer's onslaught against her.

Across the drive, Grace Ellen saw the balloon-breasted blonde girl shut her eyes as two sprays of semen liberally coated her face. Only one had been captured

on film. A moment later, as the blonde tried to see through eyes almost totally obscured with the creamy, viscous fluid, Grace Ellen gasped a last ragged exhale through the gaping wound where her throat had once been. Her vision growing dim, the last thing she was aware of was the smile on the blonde's face. Grace Ellen couldn't be sure, and she couldn't understand it, but as her consciousness flickered out she did recognize a possibility she'd never considered before.

Had the blonde actually been enjoying herself?

* * *

Emily Chassen's PT Cruiser convertible swept around a turn with just the hint of the rally wheels squealing in protest as she pulled onto the 405. The top down, she was trying to enjoy as much of the sunny Thursday mid-afternoon as possible. Weather aside, she was having a difficult go of it. She'd just downloaded her bank statement, and while the numbers were improving, they still weren't encouraging. A half-mile down the 405 she headed into the belly of the beast where the traffic wasn't encouraging, either.

"No fucking way," she exhaled. Emily knew the frustrations of the L. A. freeways as well as any Southern California driver. This, however, was totally unexpected. She had left just after noon because she knew it was the closest to empty she'd get with the 405. As the shiny, silver convertible slowed to a complete halt, a sea of stopped vehicles before her, Emily knew there must have been a cause other than the usual volume of traffic. With no accident or police vehicles in sight, Emily dropped the Cruiser into neutral and sat back, exasperated. Unless the growing tangle of traffic magically began flowing again soon, there was no way she'd make her two o'clock with Kevin at the Metro studio. Frowning at the thought of having to call up the weasely prick on her cell phone, she debated simply blowing off the meeting and making amends later. Forgetting one's cell phone in L. A. was a cardinal sin, but among "the talent," as Kevin usually referred to his actresses, it was a common occurrence.

But that wasn't going to help her bank account any, she told herself, leaving her to again curse the traffic, snarl, and slap the steering wheel in frustration. Shaking her head, she asked herself, *How the hell had she wound up here?* Emily glanced down to the passenger seat and her wide-mouthed Fendi handbag. Sticking out was the curled corner of the script she was on her way to discuss with Kevin. Foreseeing no sudden movement in the wall of traffic ahead, Emily pulled it out for a second look.

Pitiful. That's what she thought of it when she had first looked at it, and rereading it now wasn't changing her opinion any. It even looked low class, stuck into a powder blue report cover with a slip-on spine. It looked like a high school kid's senior paper, if that. Barely twenty-two pages, and that included the title page and synopsis. Thin even for a porn video. *A Hit Of Sextasy* was printed on the title page in a garish, billboard style font. Someone had been learning *Word*, Emily thought, and they weren't getting too far too fast.

There was an alternate title option they were tossing around, *Rolling On Sextasy*, but that had been dismissed when they'd handed her the script and proposal. Kevin didn't think any of the upper thirty-somethings would get the reference, and as his assistant, a mousy haired girl who looked perpetually stoned, had opined, it sounded more like a fetish flick for the fat freaks than a mainstream Sextasy Chase video. Emily believed Miss Mousy Hair was a failed break-in that Kevin was keeping around as a fluffer, likely paying her in crystal meth and using her for blowjobs after she got him his coffee and morning Vicodins. She'd seen the look in Miss Mousy Hair's eyes when she'd sat down for the meeting with Kevin, recognizing it instantly. Here she was, Miss Mousy Hair getting to see what the real Sextasy Chase was all about. Sizing her up, making comparisons. Emily knew all about that. From both sides. She'd once been Miss Mousy Hair, or someone like her, in the not-too-distant past. But that was then, this is now.

The only reason she was actually considering the offer—aside from decent, upfront money—was the dangling carrot of franchising the title as a series. That meant Emily could cash in by shooting enough intros and bumpers for about a dozen tapes. That could probably be wrapped up in about four days. As the figurehead for the series, all they'd need to bang out were a year's worth of her cameos and box cover shots. She didn't think much of the project, but it was a good-looking paycheck, and if she agreed to it the Metro guys were willing to pay her the whole nut in one lump sum.

Emily hadn't let on to anybody she was looking to get out, so by the time the year's worth of material was depleted, she'd already be gone. At least that was the plan. All she had to do was hit the goal for her retirement fund. Meaning this deal, and at least another year in the biz. That reminded her—she needed to buy Lotto tickets before Saturday night.

Emily dropped the script on the seat without completing a second read-through. She didn't need to, and she certainly didn't want to. Besides, even if she took it, which was essentially a foregone conclusion, it wasn't like they were shooting next week, and there weren't exactly a lot of lines to memorize, either. Again, the nagging voice in the back of her head—*How the hell did I get here?* Maybe there was something on the radio about the accident, or whatever it was that was tying up the traffic, Emily hoped. Anything to take her mind off *A Hit Of Sextasy*. And maybe her current bank statement, as well. She was right on both counts.

Emily turned on the radio just in time for the one o'clock traffic update. The sound of the radio station's chopper provided the background for the news.

"*Mark Price here providing continuing coverage of a situation that has the 405 backed up almost five miles. We've been following this breaking story for you for about thirty-five minutes now, as the LAPD try to neutralize two, possibly three, reanimates. Again, we've been getting conflicting reports as to whether it's two or three reanimates that have just paralyzed the southbound 405 and may also now be slowing northbound traffic as well, as police attempt to neutralize the threat to commuters.*

"*Here's a recap of what we know at this time. At approximately eleven-fifty Pacific Time, a vehicle carrying at least two passengers struck an overpass on the southbound 405. The vehicle, we have confirmed, was a 2001 Mitsubishi Montero.*

As an Emergency Medical Team unit arrived on site, they were confronted with reanimate activity and called LAPD to respond. Now, reports on what happened following that call are sketchy, but it is believed, from what we've been able to gather from independent eyewitness accounts, that the EMTs were unable to contain the reanimates at the crash site. At least one motorist who witnessed the event claims that one of the EMTs was attacked by one or more of the reanimates. Additional police have been arriving, and it is believed that they have contained the reanimates beneath the southbound overpass. Some reports on the ground have as the third reanimate that member of the EMT response team, but at this time we cannot confirm that information. We'll continue to follow the story and break in with any updates. Back to you, Stuart."

Emily already had the top on the Cruiser up and locked. The same with the doors. From the reports, she was at least two miles from the overpass where the SUV accident had occurred. Still, that was little consolation. For her money, no amount of distance between herself and a reanimate was enough to feel safe. Not truly safe, the way she had used to be able to feel, back before the whole reanimate problem had started.

Reanimates. They had even managed to come up with a politically correct term to refer to them. Unbelievable. They were zombies, for chrissakes, why did anybody feel the need to sugarcoat that? And what was the reason to call it neutralizing? Neutralizing was nothing more than a PC term for putting a bullet in their heads to end their brain function. Was it really necessary to try and make neutralization seem like it was anything else? No doubt if enough of them spoke a foreign language and were willing to work for minimum wage, the ACLU would try to secure them voting rights and access to government services. Emily fumed. The idea that there were actually those out there who wanted to find some sort of alternative to neutralization shocked her. Ever since the phenomenon had begun, the only solution had been neutralization. But now, as some people had to deal with loved ones who had become reanimates, there was a small, but vocal opposition to neutralization. Emily couldn't understand why anybody would want to prolong a person's nightmare as a reanimate. So far, while no one had been able to determine what was causing reanimation, they had learned one thing—the process did not stop natural decay. A reanimate could only cause damage as long as its shell held up. Usually that was only a matter of days. It didn't matter what the reanimate ingested, nothing seemed capable of prolonging a reanimate's span beyond the eventual biological breakdown of the creature's organs and tissues. At least that was the case for the recent dead. Those who had been embalmed and hadn't yet been interred seemed to be able to last almost indefinitely. They were the dangerous ones, but they'd become few and far between in the days after the phenomenon had been recognized. The government had now placed a temporary ban on all embalming, even though the removal and destruction of brain tissue was a matter of routine. The worldwide panic had dictated it, and no government was willing to take any chances.

Knowing there were reanimates out there, up ahead somewhere, made Emily want to turn the Cruiser around right on the side of the 405 and race up the entrance ramp the wrong way to get as far away as she possibly could. She knew that was unnecessary, bordering on the irrational, but she didn't care. Just like the government with the embalming ban, why take any chances? The reanimates themselves were irrational. They voraciously sought out human and animal flesh—as long as it was living flesh—even though they had no need for it. They had no active internal functions, aside from movement. They could not digest; they could not process anything they took in. What they ate did not pass, it simply began to decay within them, spurring on a machine of self-destructive rotting organs. It made no sense, but why should it? There was no rule that said anything had to make sense, Emily's father had explained that to her at a very young age. She'd always remembered what he'd said. Years later, she used his own words to explain why he'd disappeared, leaving her and her mother alone.

When the reanimate phenomenon first began, everybody and their brother had a theory. The religious nuts saw it as a punishment; the tree-huggers wanted to blame it all on toxic dumping, the greenhouse effect, or too many Styrofoam coffee cups. Take your pick. But when no theory seemed to find any foundation in reality, the theorists started to try and address some of the other issues. Like why former members of the human race would suddenly turn into cannibals of the living.

One guy who Emily had seen on *The O'Reilly Factor* seemed to have come up with the most logical and plausible explanation she had heard put forth thus far. He was an anthropologist, and his theory seemed to sit as well with O'Reilly as it did with Emily. He believed that the reanimates marked a return to primitivism. It was well known that throughout human history primitive peoples had engaged in the eating of their adversaries. Not for survival, but rather for power. Many primitive cultures held the belief that a person's strength could be imparted to another by eating their flesh. By ingesting your foe, you grew stronger. What are the living then, but the foes of the dead? It made sense to Emily. She hoped O'Reilly had the anthropologist on again. The longer this lasted, the more she longed for some answers she felt she could put some stock in. Lately, she had found a little of that on *O'Reilly*. She wished there were more to go around.

The blaring wail of a car horn took Emily out of her conversation with herself. She looked out ahead, half expecting to see a gap between her car and the one ahead of her. No such luck. The car in front of her had not only not moved an inch, but the driver had instead killed the engine and was now outside his vehicle, leaning on the open driver's side door, having a cigarette. He seemed oblivious to the bleating of the car horn. Emily looked around, trying to locate the source.

It only took a moment, as the honking began again the moment the driver realized that he'd caught her attention. The car was one lane to the left, and just slightly ahead of the Cruiser. The driver was a guy who looked to be in his early twenties. He was not only honking his horn, he was waving frantically, trying to get her to lower her window. Emily looked around. The only thing she saw in any of her mirrors were frustrated drivers, either sitting shut in or standing beside their cars and SUVs. No sign of imminent danger. What the hell was this guy's problem? Was one of her tires flat?

Emily lowered her window about ten inches. The mad honker was shifting his frame into his unoccupied passenger seat. As Emily was able to see more, she noticed he was talking animatedly on a cell phone.

"I knew it!" The honker was yelling into the cell phone. "Dude, it is! Yeah, right here on the 405..." He shifted attention from the cell phone and leaned out the open, passenger window. "You're Sextasy Chase! Baby, I love you! You're the finest lady in the business—there ain't nobody who can suck dick like you!"

Emily winced, then managed a weak smile. It wasn't the first time she'd been recognized, or embarrassed by one of her many, overzealous fans. It came with the territory. You don't ascend to the status of World's Number One Porn Star without going to the mall or the supermarket and not have anybody notice you. If you couldn't handle it, you shopped online and had groceries delivered. Emily had come to rely on both conveniences. The mad honker continued.

"Hey baby, when are you doing your next movie? I know a newcomer who'd work all night long with you, honey. How about it?"

Emily flashed her warmest, phoniest smile, and slowly shut the Cruiser's window, silencing the pleas of the honker. He was pleading now. "Hey baby, c'mon! Give me a chance—I got the goods, c'mon over here and give me an audition."

Dumb ass, thought Emily, watching the honker return to his cell phone. She'd run into a thousand others like him. Ten to one, even if he had anything more than a Tootsie Roll in his pants, it'd lay there limp as a noodle when the lights went on and there were eight people on the set watching. Emily had long ago graduated from having to work with untested stunt cocks. If a guy wasn't a proven performer, the odds of him getting near her, much less inside her, were zero. The only thing worse than having to endure a scene with a cherry was the occasional end of the day with a horse who was on his third or fourth wad and couldn't finish. Calling it a day with an unnecessary sore jaw, pussy, or asshole made Emily furious. It was one of the biggest reasons why she wanted out, and why she had lightened her workload the previous year.

"You know, you really don't want to back off too much," Vince Voyeur had told her recently at the Erotica Convention in New Orleans. "Jenna didn't slow up when she hit number one," he continued. "Tough to climb back once you let somebody go by you." Emily had taken Vince's advice and made it seem like she had appreciated it. In a way, she had. She respected Vince, who was now doing as much behind the camera on shoots as he did in front of it. She'd worked with Vince a few times and they'd become decent industry friends. She would have taken his advice to heart—he was one hundred percent right, of course— but he had no clue as he spoke to the recently crowned Queen of Porn, that the queen was looking to abdicate the throne.

Emily went back to the radio. Now they were confirming what she was sure some EMT's wife or girlfriend following the story at home was fearing. There had originally been only two reanimates as a result of the Montero crash. The third was now the EMT. The only good news was that the police spokesperson on the scene was confirming the neutralization was complete. *At least those three were out of their misery*, she mused, and she'd be moving again soon.

Emily was trying to tune into the *Radio Factor* when her cell phone rang. Probably Kevin, she assumed, checking to make sure that she was still coming. She

glanced at the caller ID—it was Dave Rosen over at Sextreme Sinema. She breathed a sigh of relief. Dave was a former magazine and newspaper guy from the East Coast who knew what it meant to get to the point. He'd only been in L. A. for a few years, but he'd put Sextreme on the map with a string of successful gonzo tapes. She'd done about a dozen titles for Dave, and appreciated his no-nonsense approach to making movies, if not always the product. *Ass Humpin' Angels* had been the first title she'd worked on with him, and although he wasn't as mercenary about the fucking as Max Hardcore, she'd needed several weeks off and a half tube of Preparation H before she was willing to do another anal scene. Still, Dave had been honest up front. The shoot hadn't really offered any surprises, just some real work and a little discomfort. But Dave paid her well for it and, as long as she knew up front what was going to be expected of her, she liked working for him. He had some peculiarities, but who in the business didn't? Nobody she'd ever worked with.

"Hey Dave, what's up?"

"Hi sexy, what are you up to?"

"Ugh...I'm tied up on the 405, which is probably going to kill a meeting I have this afternoon. How about you?"

"You north of that crazy zombie shit going on on TV?" Dave asked. He must have had the wide-screen in his office on.

"Yeah, you watching?"

"Yeah, everybody is. It's like *C.O.P.S.* meets *Night of the Living Dead*. Probably gone national by now. So, who you meeting with? Anybody I know?"

"Kevin over at Metro. He's got a project he wants me for. How's it look on TV? Any chance a poor little porn star is gonna get out of this mess before the real traffic starts?"

"Actually, it looks like they're reopening things now, only the two left lanes though, so get over. What's Kevin pitching?"

"Just another bullshit project, but he wants to franchise it for a year, using me as the figurehead. Why?"

"What's the rate?"

Usually, Emily wouldn't discuss what one studio was paying her for a film or project, but Dave was one of the few people on the inside she knew she could trust with the info. Besides, Dave knew most of the players anyway. She didn't doubt he could get the figure if he wanted with just a few phone calls.

"Five for the launch tape, five more for the intros for the rest of the tapes and the box shooting," she confided.

"Wanna blow it off?"

"Wanna give me a reason, besides your charming personality and a copy of *Facial Onslaught 14*?"

"No franchise, but a much better payday," Dave dangled.

"How many midgets have to cum on my face?" Emily asked facetiously. "I know you're not offering better than that for a single. What kind of money you talking about?"

"Enough to get you out, if that's what you're really wanting to do."

The response startled her. She hadn't let on to anybody who she thought would have said anything to anybody. She had discussed retirement in passing with Lauren, who was better known to the porn public as Cynful Passions, but she didn't think that would have ever gotten as far as Dave, or anybody else in the industry. Had she been a little too candid with Lauren? Had Lauren seen through some of Emily's *"someday"*'s and *"when I decide to quit"*'s and simply figured it out? Emily made a mental note—next time she and Lauren got together, smoke less pot and try to keep her mouth closed more than her legs. She hadn't fucked a guy outside a set in over a month. She was starting to feel like a full-fledged dyke.

"What makes you say that?" she asked, regretting it instantly. It had come out too aggressively. She sounded defensive.

"No reason," Dave lied, knowing she knew it. "All I can tell you right now is that I have something huge in the works here at Sextreme and I got two investment partners who agree with me. I want the biggest name in the business attached to the biggest flick since *Deep Throat* and *Behind the Green Door*. And, both of us know if we're going to do that, we have to pay accordingly. I'll tell you this, sexy, that ten grand Kevin is offering—that's not nest egg money, hon. This is."

There it was again. *Nest egg*. Another reference to her retirement. He knew, or at least suspected. The only question was how? And with this project he was pitching, how much?

"Tell you what," Emily said, finally seeing a slight bit of progress ahead of her. "Let me make a few calls and I'll swing by the office at, say, three-thirty and we can talk."

"Sounds great, sexy. While I have you on, let me ask you something. Could you work on short notice, say like tomorrow?"

"I guess that depends," Emily offered.

"On?"

"On just how nice this offer you're gonna make actually is."

Dave laughed. "I'll see you at three-thirty then. Oh, and Emily?"

"Yes?"

"Say hello to Kevin for me." Dave's end of the line went dead as the traffic started to move.

Emily Chassen had hit Los Angeles a year removed from an unsuccessful sophomore year at Penn State with the intention of taking acting lessons, trying to pay the bills with a few commercials, and partying like crazy. When her roommate decided to go back East and re-enroll at school, Emily suddenly realized her finances had hit critical mass—she was nearly out of cash, overextended on her credit cards, and on the verge of eviction from her apartment. Through her partying—the only thing she'd really succeeded in thus far—one of her friends suggested some low budget work in amateur pornos. Her friend was using that, along with a two night a week gig at a topless bar, to rake in some pretty good cash—good enough to keep her in weed and cocaine while maintaining a decent roof over her head. And no roomie, either. She set Emily up with an audition and gave her a few tips. From there, Emily was on her own. Emily didn't doubt that Monica would have continued to help her out, but an overdose had put an end to any additional assistance.

    The result was an instant name change and a crash course in the pornography industry. As Melony Chase, she had stumbled through three abominable films. First, there was *Sorority Bangin' Sisters*, in which she had one scene and had made two hundred dollars. Then there was *Co-Ed Bukkake*, where she and three other newcomers each jacked and sucked off thirty different guys, letting each one of them blow their loads on their faces. It was the most revolting thing she'd ever experienced, but she was wired on the director's coke, and the four hundred dollars she made helped her forget how close she was to eviction for another month. Her willingness to do an anal and interracial, got her two scenes in *I Sold My Soul For Anal #2*, the first flick that actually had a decent distributor behind it. By then, Emily was Melony Chase much more than she was Emily Chassen, but she was snorting enough coke to keep her from caring very much about the difference.

    The payday on *Sold My Soul* wasn't enough to pay for the work that the director had suggested, but he made her an offer. He'd front the money for a two cup increase breast augmentation and some collagen work on her lips in return for two scenes in each of his next three videos. Needing the money, even though it wasn't all that much, and feeling the cosmetic changes couldn't hurt, she agreed. Melony Chase disappeared under the surgeon's blade, and Sextasy Chase was born.

    By the time the third video was released, Sextasy Chase was fast becoming a hot commodity. With Jenna Jameson retired, the industry was looking for the next XXX-rated superstar. With a torrid schedule doing videos for Vivid, Metro, Extreme, and some of the other heavyweights, in less than a year she had become one of the hottest stars in the business. She made the cover of *Adult Video News* with the coverline: "Is Sextasy the Next Jenna J.?" That, and hitting the covers of *CHERI* and *High Society* in back to back months—something even Jenna hadn't done—sealed it. *CHERI*'s Ken Kimmel had been one of the first to recognize Jenna's superstar potential, and now nobody in the industry was missing the significance of Sextasy's unprecedented sweep of the two powerhouse skin mags. She was the industry's undisputed number one star.

    Now, less than two years later, she was looking for a way out. A near miss with her own drug overdose had shaken her up. That, coupled with her mother's advanced Alzheimer's, made her departure all the more imminent. She woke up some mornings and asked her reflection, *"When did it go from teenage stupidity to being a fucked out whore?"*

    Her relationship with Lauren had helped. In her she saw the girl she'd once been, but with one notable difference—Lauren wasn't interested in getting out. Nothing she saw or endured in the business seemed to change her outlook. Emily thought it was because of Lauren's background. Lauren dismissed it, but one didn't get dropped off at a Catholic boarding school by your mother at age twelve, only to have her disappear and never pick you up without it screwing you up in some way or another. Lauren denied it, but some things she said, or occasionally cried out in her restless sleep, made Emily suspect that the nuns at St. Barbara's had done far worse things with a ruler than just smack Lauren's knuckles raw. Outside the business, Lauren was frail and scared. Inside, she was powerful and successful. She didn't want to test herself outside the industry. She didn't see any reason to leave, and she didn't have the courage to look for one.

Emily refused to feel guilty about making the call. Lauren finally answered on the fifth ring, still somewhat asleep. Emily could only imagine what Lauren was up to the night before if it was approaching two in the afternoon and she hadn't found her way out of bed yet.

"Hey doll, I was just having the nastiest wet dream about you. Why don't you come over and I'll see how nasty it really was in person?"

"Sorry, darling, I've got a meeting in a little bit. I just wanted to let you know that you should call Kevin at Metro because he needs a sexy-fine lady and your name is on the tip of his tongue," Emily responded. She hoped Lauren wasn't too out of it to pull herself together and secure the Metro gig Emily had just turned down.

"Really? What happened? I thought you were going to meet with them about something."

"I bailed," admitted Emily. "The offer was nice, but I just didn't want to commit to it. But they still have a hole in their schedule, so I told Kevin that *Simply Cynful* sounded like a good idea. What do you think?"

"Ooh, I like it. When does he need to talk about it?"

"Since you're in his neck of the woods, I told him to give you an hour. Can you manage that?"

"*Ouch*. Tight, but then again, so am I. Yeah, I can make it. What about you? Why'd you dump the Metro gig?"

"You know, I'm not even sure, really. Dave at Sextreme called, said he had something he wanted to get me on board for. Promised to make it worth my while, so I figure if he says it's gonna be better than Metro money, I get to make him live up to it."

"That, sister, is good thinking. They must have something really good going. They closed the studio down yesterday, moved the last few scenes of *Cum Freaks* to that ranch house they rent out in the canyons. For them to do that they must really have something hot going. No surprise they want to get you in on it. Did you know that the last volume of *Cum Freaks* outsold the last *Gag Factor* and *Creme de la Face*?"

"No, but I'm not surprised. Dave seems to really know his shit. Anyway, take Kevin for every penny he's got, sweetie. I'll talk to you soon."

Emily didn't want to admit it to herself but, deep inside, some part of her knew the truth. She hadn't just handed her friend a plum. It was more like a good-bye present.

Sextreme Sinema was one of the few production companies that actually spent the money to maintain both a decent office in town and an actual working studio. The studio was the very last building in the corner of a commercial park located on the outskirts of L.A., in what had once been a fly-by-night rap record label's base of operations. Dave was ecstatic when he found the place. He'd hardly had to spend a dime to turn it into an instantly functional stage for shooting porn videos. He'd worked out a sweetheart deal with the realtor, who'd bent over backwards trying to find a tenant for whom he didn't have to subdivide or compromise on renovation money.

With a lot of the shooting taking place at night, when half the commercial park was empty, the studio doubled as an out of the way party space any time a shoot wrapped. Dave had had to grease the wheels a little bit with his partner Brian, who had been planning quite the bash for the wrap on *Cum Freaks 14*. The title was Sextreme's jewel, their most profitable franchise. Renting out the canyon property was an olive branch, and the extra two thousand dollars Dave had thrown in cash for "party favors" made Brian feel a lot better about getting bounced. Dave expected that Brian might bust his balls a little when it came to the budget for the next *Cum Freaks*, but it didn't bother him any. If he could swing Emily for this one video, the money Sextreme had spent on all of its releases this year and the year before would be negligible. He was poised to make the most incredible porn flick ever, and having to free up the studio was the least of his concerns. He'd been working the phones non-stop since just after one in the morning, when he came up with the idea with T.J., his studio production manager. He'd instantly gone into overdrive, calling in his two original investment partners and offering them a piece of the action if they could come up with six figures each. By noon, just before he'd called Emily, the cash had shown up in the Sextreme coffers via wire transfer.

As Dave pulled around the studio building, to the narrow, largely unlit parking strip in the back, he strategized how he was going to handle his superstar. He hadn't heard her deny his insinuations about her retiring once during their phone conversation, at least, not convincingly. Dave knew he'd guessed right, Emily was looking to get out. She'd been talking to his friend Anneli Adolffson about doing some more print work, which she certainly didn't need—unless she was looking to stockpile cash for some reason. Anneli even thought she could get Emily onto the sexkittens.com Web site, something she hadn't been able to get Sextasy to consider before. Dave knew Emily had backed off the coke and was only rarely smoking pot any more. The brush with the overdose had really cleaned up Emily's act. That left bad legal trouble, which he knew Emily didn't have, or hoarding a nest egg. He was sure it was the latter.

Dave got out of his Escalade and walked to the back entrance. He noticed some small pieces of glass as he walked past their dumpster. He'd have to have T.J. come out and clean that up, and maybe see if there was anything he could do about the freshly laid skidmark there. No reason to leave the area like that.

Inside, the air conditioning was going full blast. Any other day and he'd think it was bordering on freezing. He checked his watch—it was three-eighteen. Perfect. Emily was always on time. All he'd have to do now was convince her to take the money.

T.J. appeared from the prop room, looking like warmed over dog shit. He was unshaved, and even with the frigid air, big sweat rings were evident under his arms and the neck of his tee shirt. Dave could tell instantly that T.J. hadn't slept; he hadn't used anything as a pick-me-up, either. T.J. walked over and yawned.

"Any problem with the fridge company?" Dave asked his haggard right hand man.

"Nope. Little pricey, but on such short notice..."

"Where is it?"

"I had them put it on the other side of the prop room, where it wouldn't look too out of place. Told them we were filming beer commercials the next two weeks."

"Nice," commented Dave. T.J. was the best production manager he'd ever had on a staff, and it was on days like today that Dave was reminded why he paid him as well as he did. You got what you paid for, especially in this industry, Dave understood, and T.J. was well worth every penny.

"Everything else is all ready to roll, all we need is the go ahead. I got the tightest crew we know, skeletonized, if you'll pardon the expression. Bare bones all the way."

"Good. Why don't you show me the set-up and knock off for the day. If I get the word, I'll call you on the cell. Keep it close...time's a factor."

"You got it. Think she'll go for it?" asked T.J., leading Dave to where T.J. had instructed the refrigeration company to set up a huge cooling unit for the shoot.

"Christ, what a behemoth. This a little more than we need for our...uh, beer?"

"Yeah, I know. First thing I thought was 'overkill,' but when you need something at two in the morning for a shoot, you're kinda limited on the available options. So, you think you can sign her?"

"I think so," Dave responded with confidence. "Have you ever known a porn actress to ever turn down this kind of money for any sex act?"

"Not even close," T.J. responded. Standing near the rear exit, both men heard the sound of a car pulling up.

"I'd love to stay and hear this," lamented T.J., tugging at his filthy T-shirt. "But..."

"No, go on, get some rest."

T.J. grinned wide. "Man," he laughed, "this is gonna be the most crazy, fucked-up shoot I've ever worked on."

"No shit. Hey, when you leave, take a look by the dumpster, ok?"

"Will do." T.J. pulled out his key ring, and slipped out through the emergency exit at the back of the prop room. Dave headed for the rear studio entrance, where he let Emily in.

It was three-twenty nine.

T.J. caught just a glimpse of blonde hair and firm, round ass disappearing through the studio door as he slipped through the emergency exit. He'd seen ten thousand naked chicks in his years working on pornos, but he still had something for this one. There was a reason she had burst upon the scene and been instant gold. Bigger than Chasey Lane, hotter than Kobe Tai, hotter than even the legendary Jenna. Years from now, he thought, scooping up some remnants of broken glass he'd been unable to see in the wee hours the night before, they would be writing articles about her the way they had about Traci Lords. He wondered, given the way things were, if she could possibly become *more* infamous. Tossing the last of the broken glass into the dumpster, he doubted it. Minutes later, cruising out of the commercial park in his Durango, he wondered if there was any chance that he'd be able to get any sleep at all. He doubted that, too.

"Holy shit, Dave, it's a meat locker in here," Emily remarked, stepping into the studio. "You doing an Eskimo fuck flick in here or something?"
"No, not quite, hon. Come on into my office, it's a little warmer in there."
Dave led her to the small office he kept at the studio. It was sparse, little more than four sheetrock walls painted a dull, sour-milk grey. Eggshell, the can had said. Dave wouldn't cook an egg this color if he were starving. The furniture consisted of a simple desk, leather chair, computer, and two office chairs for guests. Usually this was where T.J. would do his paperwork, filing copies of model releases, photo IDs, and HIV/AIDS clearance tests. When Dave was on set, it was his office, but for all intents and purposes it was T.J.'s command center.
"Something to drink?" Dave offered, pulling a bottle of iced tea from T.J.'s small fridge.
"No thanks," Emily declined. Dave thought she looked a little bit antsy. Was it because she was trying to determine if he was as sure as he was that she was eyeing early retirement, or was she just anxious to get down to business and see why she had left Kevin at Metro hanging on the franchise deal?
"So," she started. "What have you got lined up that's worth me giving up ten grand just to meet with you here in the tundra?"
Dave sat down in his chair and looked at Emily over the desk. He went right after her. "You're looking to get out, aren't you?"
"What are you talking about?" Emily asked half-heartedly. Dave knew he'd been right the moment the words had tumbled out of her mouth. He felt he was halfway home.
"C'mon. Last year me, the guys at Metro, Leisure Time, Vivid, everybody is knocking down your door. You did what, fifteen videos last year? Now, you're working every two weeks like you just started making movies, and for anybody who has the cash. You sit there and tell me that you're not looking to get out."
Emily wasn't going to lie to Dave, one of the few legit friends she had in the industry. Slowly, she nodded. "Yeah," she heard herself admit. "I'm thinking about it."
"How close are you? How long you think you have until you're ready?"
"A year, maybe a little less...Depends on the paydays between now and September," she told him.
"September?" Dave followed up. "Why September?"
"Believe it or not, tax problems."
"Em, if you have—"
"No, not my problems. At least, not technically. My mother's in an assisted living place now. She seems to have let a whole lot of years go by without paying any property tax on the house I grew up in. She owes a hundred thousand and change on it. My accountant says I can get everything cleared up free and clear for about eighty thousand. I want to be able to cover that and have at least another

hundred in the bank until I decide what I want to do next. I can live off the merchandise, autographed stuff, and the Web site for a while, but the longer I'm gone, well, you know. They're not gonna care about me forever."

Dave reflected on what she had said for a moment, let the air between them hang empty while he chose his words. "What if I told you I could get you six figures if you only do one more flick and I could guarantee the money to you in twelve hours?"

"I'd say you were crazy, but I'd give you the twelve hours."

"Come on inside," suggested Dave, rising. "I want to show you something."

Dave led a skeptical Emily back into the studio. The wide open area was familiar to her, she'd done most of her work for Sextreme here. The last time she'd been here had been for *Sextasy and the City*, where she'd delivered such vapid and ridiculous lines as, "Do you really want to meet a nice guy and settle down, or do you just wanna date guys who know how to really give you a good ass fuck?" It had been a video she'd done with Lauren, who did a good job in the bitchy Kim Cattrall role, while Emily struggled to mimic Sarah Jessica Parker's tics and mannerisms. After watching several episodes of the cable program being mimicked, she wondered why anybody would want to see either version. Both were pieces of shit.

Emily shivered as Dave walked her past the prop room. The studio must have purchased some new equipment, she mused, taking note of the enormous, steel storage locker that hadn't been there during the *City* shoot.

"Is there anybody in the business you wouldn't work with, Em? I mean, if the money was right?"

"I wouldn't relish the idea of having to do a scene with Rodney Moore," Emily offered. Rodney was legendary in the biz for torrential facials—geysers of cum that literally swamped girls' faces. "But like you said, if the money was right. But I'm not working with Max Hardcore for anything. I'm not letting him piss in my ass and stretch me big enough to get a wide angle up my pussy for anything."

"How about this then, what if I told you I'll deposit two hundred thousand dollars into your bank account, available before we even turn on the lights, and all you have to do is one scene, one we can bang out tomorrow."

"Two hundred thousand for one scene? Since I doubt you can line up a girl-girl with Britney Spears and the 'N Sync guy thrown in for shits and giggles, who do you want me to work with?"

Dave smiled, and opened the huge steel door to what Emily had assumed was a secure storage container. The gust of ice cold air that rushed out chilled her skin. But what chilled her to the core was what she saw through the fog of artificially frigid air. Standing there in the shadow of the doorway, chained to a steel ring, was a reanimate.

Emily jumped back a step in spite of the chains around the reanimate's waist and legs.

"*No fucking way...*" gasped Emily. "*You can't possibly think—*" She refused to finish her own sentence. He wasn't kidding. This was the reason he cleared his most profitable series out to the canyon. This was why he knew he could play her against the deal at Metro. Two hundred thousand dollars. He was as serious as a heart attack. He wanted her to fuck a corpse.

Emily wanted to turn away, but just like the morbid rubberneckers who slowed to stare at the carnage of a car accident, she couldn't.

The reanimate wasn't a staffer she recognized, even though he was wearing a Sextreme Sinema T-shirt. There was a huge bloodstain on the shoulder, and an equally large stain right in the center of his chest, from which a piece of what looked like steering wheel protruded. As Emily took in the gruesome details, the reanimate shuffled forward a few inches. It was the most he could move while chained. As he turned his head slightly, Emily could see the source of the bloodstain that marked his shoulder. The crown of his head on the right side was caved in. Emily winced. The reanimate was having difficulty orienting his head, likely due to whatever damage the obvious car accident had caused, but when the poor soul did finally adjust his mangled frame enough to view Emily his demeanor changed noticeably. His eyes widened as his hands rose. He was reaching out towards her. Emily stiffened.

He recognized her.

"Who is he?" Emily finally managed, "And what happened to him?"

"I don't think it's important to know his name," said Dave. "Easier if you didn't, probably. You never met him, he's only been working for us for about a month. He knew T.J., and as you can see, he was looking to get into the business on the other side of the camera."

Emily had been mesmerized by the nameless reanimate's face and his horrible wounds. Now, after Dave had alerted her, she let her eyes drift downward. She was shocked. The chain around the reanimate's waist held him in place, but it wasn't secured through his belt loops as Emily had assumed. No, the chain was wrapped around bare flesh, and when Emily looked carefully, she could see the dark impressions the links had left in the reanimate's cold skin. Beneath that, the reanimate's pants were pushed halfway down his thighs, revealing a massive erection, easily nine inches in length, dark and engorged with trapped blood. Blood that no longer knew to leave his cock. It was easy for Emily to make out the discolored outline of the reanimate's grip—the spots where his fingers had been tightly clutching his enormous erection, you could practically make out his fingerprints. It was eerie, and reminded Emily of those cable TV detective shows she often watched. Programs that showed women who'd been strangled to death who had been found with similar marks on their throats. Just past the foremost mark on his shaft, there was an unnatural bend in his dick. Emily began piecing a likely scenario of his demise in her head. Without asking, Dave confirmed much of her amateur guesswork. All those Tuesday nights watching *FBI Files* and the *New Detectives* on the Discovery Channel had been worthwhile after all.

"It happened early this morning, after everybody but T.J. had wrapped and headed home. We think he was driving out of the lot and couldn't wait to get back to his apartment to get off. Can't blame him. Yesterday we had Jette Black in shooting her last scene for *Cum Freaks*. You remember her? She was the one I used for *I Love Loosie* and *PokeHerHotAss*. Girl's a fucking throat goddess. She's also a terrible flirt. She had the kid running around for her all shoot. 'Can you get me a water, sweetheart? Bring me my cell phone? Would you make me happy and get me the baggie in my purse?' That sort of shit. He probably walked out of here ready to screw his own belly button."

"It's hardly lit back there at night," Emily recalled aloud.

"Yeah, I know. We think he was driving out with one hand on the wheel and took his eyes off the lot. When T.J. heard the crash, he ran out and saw it was already too late. He called me—I was only about ten minutes away myself. We brought him in and locked him up. Had him in the deep freeze less then three hours later. Aside from his head and his chest..."

Emily heard how easily Dave was slipping into the pitch. "He's a fucking zombie, Dave, a fucking dead guy."

"And, he's a big fan of yours," Dave added. "He was jacking off to your most recent *CHERI* layout when he drove into the dumpster back there. Look at the fucking guy—he's got one foot in the grave and you and I both know he knows it. And he can *still* tell it's you. He isn't even looking at me. Last night T.J. and I were nothing more than human happy meals to him, but look, look at him now. Any minute and he's gonna try and finish what he started in his car last night." Emily was listening to Dave, but matching stares with the reanimate. She thought Dave was right—this reanimate wasn't going crazy, like the ones she'd seen those first days on the news. He wasn't tearing at the chains. He was simply standing there, like a puppy at the end of his leash. As Emily watched, the reanimate looked like he was trying to say something to her, something reanimates weren't capable of because their lungs and diaphragms no longer functioned. Eventually, he settled on a crooked smile, and reached for his twisted erection. At that, Emily turned away.

"Two hundred thousand big ones, Em. You know, the word is that the Japs are going to do one, it's just a matter of time. If not them, then the Germans. You know what kind of sick fucks those guys are. They've been making dog films and shit movies and enema torture flicks with teenage girls and amputees. We do this, and you'll never have to do another video ever again."

"No, I - that's different...This is just..." Emily was struggling for words now. She wanted out. She needed to get out, more than Dave knew. But this, this was beyond anything she'd ever thought of. Before her first amateur film she'd once done some escorting. It was a lousy, low-budget service on the fringes of L.A. She'd never told anybody about it, it was a two month black hole that she had consciously cut out of her life. Not even Lauren, who'd confessed all sorts of personal tragedies to her, knew about Emily's time there. While she had been in the tightest grips of her coke habit, she had found herself doing things for money that she would never discuss. Unspeakable things...degrading things, depraved things...painful things. There were the services that catered to powerful businessmen who simply wanted high class, discrete fucking. And then there was a whole other side, the services where anything goes, where some men paid thousands to put cigars out in your asshole and use a stun gun on your clit. There were Johns who demanded that you puncture the skin of their ass with knitting needles like their mother had done because they had been bad—as bad as they had been when they were five and mommy needed to teach them a lesson. And there were guys who needed to know what it was like to cum in your ass while they were choking you into unconsciousness.

These "clients" didn't understand the meaning of the word "no," and they paid extra not to hear it behind closed doors. Emily knew all that. She knew it all too well. She thought about her mom, the house in Pennsylvania that was so close to slipping away. She was never going to be back in that situation again, that she had promised herself the last night she escorted. The night of the overdose, the night she'd failed.

"Em, what do you think is next? What happens when you've done all the stuff the straight guys want to see? Are you going to want to do double interracial penetration videos with guys like Mr. Marcus and Sean Michaels tearing you up so bad you'd need diapers when you're forty? Are you going to be willing to go back to gonzo movies? Having three hundred guys blowing loads on your face while you wear a plastic dog collar and they feed you the overflow with a scoop? Are you going to let somebody gag you with their cock until you barf in his crotch just because they can market it in Amsterdam and Germany? How many more videos do you think you have in you before you have to start doing the edgy, exploitative shit? Lizzy Borden's already tapping into kidnap, rape and phony snuff. Do you want to hang around that long?"

Emily didn't notice it, but she was shaking. Dave was right, across the board. Anything less than three and four-ways and companies weren't interested, not at her full rate. Even at Metro, Kevin had brought up an anal threesome with guys hung like donkeys. Guys she'd remember fucking for days, with constant reminders every time she went to the bathroom. Dave's question hung in the air, unanswered. *How long did she want to hang around?*

"If I say yes," Emily asked, "how long until the money is in my account?"

"The bank is offshore. It's still early enough to make a transfer. It wouldn't take long at all. We could do the shooting tonight. How about in four hours?"

"Make it two," demanded Emily, not willing to allow herself the time to back out. "And you've got yourself Sextasy Chase in her last starring role."

T.J. got the call, interrupting a brief, half-hour's worth of sleep. He was still slightly surprised that Dave had been able to seal the deal, but that was Dave—he knew how to run things, he knew what he wanted, and he had an uncanny ability to get it.

The next two hours were a blur. Getting together the members of his skeleton crew, and getting them out to the studio took only about an hour. As they set up, Dave was making the electronic bank transfer and alternately quelling any concerns Emily continued to have.

Dave put out the fires as soon as they flared. When Emily grew concerned about the reanimate's taste for flesh, Dave informed her that they'd had a dentist who did all the work for Sextreme's talent. Dave knew the value of a nice set of choppers, particularly when there was so much cocksucking getting filmed, so he had a dentist on stand-by, much the same way he had a cosmetic surgeon on retainer for instant, moment's notice boob jobs and emergency liposuction. Sextreme was a machine whose wheels were greased with cum, cash and cunt juice. Dave was a master at keeping his machine rolling efficiently with generous amounts of all three.

T.J. was rooting around in the office for a new digital video lens and Dave took the cue to let his star have a few minutes to get ready. With some production details to take care of while the transfer of funds was taking place, he excused himself.

"You almost ready?" asked T.J. "The guys can't wait to get rolling."

"I will be, as soon as I know the financial end is tied up. I'm not really looking forward to this one, T.J., this one's mercenary. This is the one that really makes me a whore. This is one hundred percent about the money."

"Nothing wrong with mercenary, babe. Get yours while the getting's good. This industry doesn't have any union, no benefits package, no pensions. When you're time's up, it isn't going to feel it owes you anything, so there's nothing wrong with being mercenary. Wring every last buck out of the bitch."

Emily laughed. "Thanks, T.J. That's the best I've felt about this decision all day."

"You feeling okay otherwise? If you want..." T.J. reached into the top drawer of the desk and took out a little black cylinder. A 35mm film canister. He didn't need to say anything. Emily's eyes widened. She had been thinking of clearing her head for a while now. T.J. was already at the door, lens in hand.

"If you want, it's there. Help yourself." Before she could say thanks, T.J. was out of there, the door closing behind him.

T.J. paused, fumbled with the lens, which nobody had asked for and the crew didn't need. Before he'd taken another step, he heard the unmistakable sound of a deep sniff.

Just as Dave had predicted.

T.J. gave Dave the thumbs-up immediately upon leaving the office. Dave would give her two minutes before he went in and told her what he'd just confirmed via cell phone—the two-hundred-thousand dollars had been successfully transferred. Now, she was his—there was no backing out.

Dave hated lying to Emily. She was one of the few cunts-for-hire he genuinely liked. Not like that whore Jette Black, who was so busy fluffing Danny the freezer boy for hits out of his film vial that they'd wound up wrapping after one in the morning. Dave had been furious that T.J. had to call him down to the studio to get involved. The director, Peter Bowne, was so coked up he had no control over the set. It took Dave's presence to whip the crew into shape and finish the day's shooting. Dave then told Bowne to finish the shoot in the canyon because he didn't want any heat to come down on Sextreme's property. He also laid it on the line to the director of his most successful franchise that he wanted Jette to get, ". . . face-fucked like she deserved, paid, and off the canyon property before her face even dries. I never want to see that skank on a Sextreme production again. And if this crew doesn't shape up," Dave added, noting no exceptions, "they won't work a Sextreme production ever again...Any of them." The message sent, Dave was discussing with T.J. what to do about Danny, the new assistant P.A., when they heard the squeal of brakes, followed by rubber straining against the pavement, and then a glass crunching crash.

"Great, just what we need," fumed Dave as he'd walked alongside D.J. to the back door. "How fucked up is this kid? I don't want any accident report being filed tonight if he's wrecked."

"He's a fucking mess," T.J. had informed Dave, "He wasn't even phased when I fired him. He was going to go hook up with Jette at the Lizard Lounge. I think he was selling as much blow as he was using. Little cocksucker was probably looking to get in just for the hook up with the tail. I don't doubt it. The ratbastard even—Holy shit!..."

They had come upon Danny's 2002 Lexus, which was pinned beneath the sharp slant of the dumpster. The air bag had gone off and looked like it had broken the punk's neck.

Dave was steamed. "Dumb fucking bag of shit. What a goddamn mess. No way we're letting this douche bag call the cops or the insurance company tonight."

"Wanna leave him here to choke on his own puke?" suggested T.J.

"Much as I'd like to, that idiot Jette would probably come back looking for her coke-daddy and freak. Let's drag the putz inside and roll the car all the way in the back so nobody can see it."

It was nothing Emily would ever know, but Dave was reliving it moment by moment as he approached the office door.

T.J. and Dave were trying to figure out what to do with the coked out, semi-conscious ex-P.A., when the kid started shaking. As Dave and T.J. stood over him, Danny writhed and convulsed furiously.

"*Shit*," snarled T.J. "You want me to call Rodriguez?" He was referring to Dr. Manuel Rodriguez, who had been known to treat, quite discretely, the not-so-rare overdose on a porn set. He might have had a sheepskin from an uncredited school in the Philippines, but the son of a bitch sure knew his drugs. He probably had killed as many L.A. girls as he'd saved with his painkiller "prescriptions," but at least he was reliable.

"What if we just leave him there on the floor?" mused Dave. "I really don't want to call Manny up, much less pay him for this loser."

The question had been rhetorical, but it was late, and T.J. took it and ran with it. Jokingly, he suggested, "He croaks, we wire his jaw shut and then find some crackwhore to fuck him for a hundred bucks and a baggie of crystal meth."

"You know," Dave opined as Danny's legs continuing to jerk and tremble, "that's pretty fucking brilliant. I bet we could market that, call it, *Fuck of the Living Dead*."

"Not bad" chuckled T.J., "I think we could do better, though."

The hour was getting to them. Foamy spittle was starting to leak out of Danny's mouth.

"*Babe-E-us Corpus*?" Dave suggested. T.J. moaned. Danny's head began pounding against the concrete floor as the convulsions grew worse.

"Will you look at that? I've never seen anything quite like this."

"This is the kind of shit you only see on those cable medical programs. I should probably be taping it," answered T.J.

"So, what if he doesn't croak?" Dave looked his right hand man in the eye.

"I dunno. What are you thinking?"

"Maybe we should make sure."

T.J. knew that the conversation had progressed beyond idle fantasy into a legitimate *"what if"* scenario. He weighed the proposal. "We could whack the fuck. We cut the air bag and the Lexus is drivable. We leave that thing on the street a half mile up the road it's as good as gone."

"Why don't you get on the horn, see if you can't get us a small, commercial fridge. Something solid. I'm going to make a few calls. I think this might work, if we get the right chick to fuck this shitbag," Dave said.

"Got anybody in mind?" asked T.J. while duct taping Danny's arms and legs together like the mummy. His head was now banging against the floor at a tempo that would have impressed Buddy Rich.

"What about Sextasy Chase?" said Dave.

At first, T.J. laughed.

"The number one porn star in the world, instead of a crack whore?"

"Sure, why not," answered Dave, already dialing his cell phone, his mind racing. He looked down at the frothing, convulsing drug casualty on the floor. "If we're gonna make history, why not go all the way?"

Dave rapped on the door before he went inside. Emily's face had taken on a pink, rosy glow. Dave was satisfied—she was higher than she'd likely been in months. She was probably more than ready to spread those golden thighs for some corpse cock, but he figured he'd give her the news she wanted to hear just to make her one hundred percent.

"Good news, love. The transfer is complete. If you want to log on and check your much improved balance, you have my computer at your disposal."

"That sounds like a plan. Let me check this out and we can get rolling, okay?"

Dave smiled a wide, genuine smile. "Sounds like we're gonna make a movie," he agreed. "The crew will be ready when you are."

T.J. had the crew in place and waiting. As soon as Sextasy was satisfied her cash was in place, he and Jack Terrell, an ex-con he'd used for some set building and other odd studio jobs, would get Danny out of the deep freeze and hope the recently deceased addict could be coerced into actually pulling this off. Terrell knew what the deal was and didn't give a shit. He'd done seven years for a manslaughter in the early nineties and knew T.J. through T.J.'s own extensive coke connections. Jack didn't know shit about the movie business, but he knew how to keep his mouth shut for two large a night, and tonight that's exactly what T.J. wanted out of him. That, and somebody good with their own snub-nosed .38, in case Danny boy got out of hand. On that front, Jack was also their man. He didn't like reanimates, and even though he wasn't thrilled about being around one, the .38, and the amateur dentistry made taking the two thousand in cash that much easier.

T.J. snuck a look over at the freezer. They had the door open again, keeping Danny chilled, but allowing him to thaw enough to be able to move. T.J. hoped they'd gotten all the teeth. He knew the line of bullshit Dave had fed Sextasy. The two of them had actually done the job themselves with a pair of pliers. Thinking back on it, T.J. thought it was a pair of channel locks, but that didn't matter much. That was just one part of this whole fucking fiasco he was going to put out of his mind when he took a few weeks off in Tahiti, smoking unbelievable weed and fucking natural, cocoa-skinned native girls who didn't know what implants were. They had had a horrible time of it at first with Danny's teeth, the first two breaking off in pieces, leaving jagged shards sticking out of his receding gums. It seemed Danny hadn't been much of a milk drinker as a kid. After wrestling with the jutting shards of enamel, they had gradually gotten better, learning to crush each tooth less as they tore them out of the kid's jaw, twisting them out the further back they went towards the molars. Those had been tough, but eventually, they got them out, too. Dave had remarked happily that Danny didn't have any wisdom teeth. The lack of extra work was a plus.

What had made the initial extractions more difficult was the fact that Danny had still been alive when they had started, although this was unknown to both T.J. and Dave at the time. It had been almost fifteen minutes since Danny had stopped writhing, and it hadn't seemed like the kid was breathing. Two teeth in, Danny's eyes shot open and he had started screaming. T.J. knew he'd never be able to smoke that out of his mind, no matter how good the weed or how much of it he smoked. No, that was one he was going to be stuck with for the long haul and he was just going to have to learn to live with it. At least he wasn't going to have the additional burden Dave was saddled with. Dave had run into the prop room when Danny's high-pitched screams had begun and come back with a piece of steel pipe—a remnant left over from some previous plumbing work done for the rap studio. The hip-hop hotshots had installed a jacuzzi for their pampered, second tier artists. Now, it was occasionally used to weigh down extra lighting equipment. It took four shots to Danny's head to do the job. T.J. had always believed one good shot with a bat or pipe would crack open a skull, but Danny's head held up pretty well against the first three blows. It was only on the fourth swing that the top of the kid's skull cracked like an egg and dented inward. T.J. had never been so happy that the studio had a slop sink and bucket. Danny was one leaky motherfucker. There had been a lot for Dave and him to mop up.

The studio went silent when Sextasy opened the door and emerged from the office. Lucy, the stylist, had dressed Sextasy in a sexy, red mini dress with no bra and no panties underneath. Her tits looked outstanding. The dress was probably better fitted for a 34C cup, and Sextasy was a very full 36D, verging on DD. All the extra tit up front pulled the ass of the mini dress up, so it barely covered her cheeks. It was Lucy's hope that when Sextasy got into position and spread for Danny, no matter how uncoordinated he was, not having to fumble with any undergarments would enable him to just plow right in. Lucy had already generously swabbed Sextasy's snatch with Astroglide—she knew Sextasy wasn't going to lubricate naturally for this. At least Lucy had hoped she wouldn't. Personally, Lucy found the whole thing an abomination. But she was getting a thousand bucks for it.

"Places, everybody!" ordered T.J., scrambling the crew into motion. It was a good, tight crew. They knew about getting things right, especially on the first take. A lot of times that was all you got, especially if you were shooting a good facial.

Nobody liked having to wait around for a guy to reload, and nobody wanted a dribbler for the money shot. Tonight, T.J. had told the whole crew to be on top of their shit. This was definitely a one-take scene. The bonus was that all they had to worry about was the action. There weren't going to be any crazy camera angles for DVD, no stop-and-go, no changing positions. And, no money shot.

Dave was still buttering his star actress up as she strode out in front of the lights. The director of photography did a color balance on both of the DV cams they were rolling and snapped his fingers for sound. They were live, and he gave the okay. They were ready.

Dave walked Sextasy all the way to her spot and encouraged her, "This is gonna go perfect, honey. You just play this like any other scene, okay? Just pretend it's any other guy and it'll be over before you know it. All right?"

The best she could do was nod. Not a good sign, as Dave was really counting on her to provide some audio fireworks. Not only was she the best blowjob queen and ass-fuck in the biz, she was also a great screamer. Dave was hoping her silence would be short-lived once the cameras were rolling.

For the scene, they'd kept everything simple aside from the set. For that, they'd dragged their kitchen backdrop and props alongside a living room flat. Jack had tapped a few nails here and there, and the whole thing looked pretty seamless. The idea was to shoot Sextasy playing with herself in the kitchen, waiting for her boyfriend to arrive. When she was on the verge of orgasm, a knock would come from off camera and she'd go to the kitchen door. There, Jack would have Danny ready. He'd slapped together some boards, effectively penning Danny up like a bull at a rodeo waiting to come out of the chute. The hope was that the horny fuck would follow Sextasy through the kitchen and into the living room. There, Sextasy would fall back over the arm of the couch, giving Danny the chance he had missed with Jette Black the night before. That's how everybody hoped it would work.

"Quiet...rolling...action," said T.J., viewing the taping on a dual monitor set-up just off the living room set. Like a true professional, Sextasy went right to it.

In her head, Sextasy was trying to play it like any other scene. She had all the mechanics down, this wasn't anything she hadn't done a thousand times before.

"Where the hell can he be?" she heard herself ad libbing. "I can't believe he's not here yet, and my pussy is so fucking wet!" Without thinking, she started to caress her breasts. Dave and T.J. watched the monitor approvingly. So far, vintage Sextasy. Even with only lipstick and a little rouge, she looked absolutely phenomenal.

Sextasy started increasing the tempo, and the heat. Now she was gripping her breasts tightly, teasing the camera, tugging down the dress just enough to expose the tops of her nipples. With the set being so cold, they were bright pink and jutting out like small thimbles.

One hand slipped down to the hemline of the dress, tugging it out and up just enough to reveal a hint of pussy fuzz. Sextasy had pulled the top of the dress down enough to free one magnificent tit, which she was now tugging to her mouth, engulfing her erect nipple between her thick, painted lips. A strand of saliva—Sextasy could drool like no other actress—glistened as it trickled down her boob.

Guys will be jacking off just to this, thought Dave. T.J. looked up, and tapped a spot on the monitor.

Sextasy had one finger buried inside herself and was thrusting her hips forward against her hand. The whole top of her dress was folded down now, and both her tits were exposed, heaving as she finger-fucked herself. As her moaning grew louder, Dave leaned in to see what T.J. was trying to point out to him. It was obvious, once Dave saw it. T.J. cupped a hand to Dave's ear. "He's fucking watching her. You can see him through the kitchen door window staring at her. How cool is that?"

Dave didn't need to answer. It appeared neither of his actors required any direction.

"Oh, I wish he'd hurry up and get here already," whined Sextasy, sticking her pussy-prodding fingers into her mouth and sucking them noisily. "I need it so bad!"

T.J. put his hand up over his head and spun one finger in the air. Jack took the cue, and rapped his knuckles on the outer wall of the set.

Sextasy took the cue and made it appear that she was reluctant to stop sucking her fingers. She slowly pulled her dress back up, pressing her tits together as she did so, working it for the camera. She grabbed an empty purse from the countertop and strode to the door. Nobody noticed that she was walking on wobbly legs.

Danny went for her the moment she opened the door. He had a hand wrapped around his erection, now so dark it was turning purple-black. Another six hours, he'd be able to do his own interracial scene.

Dave was astounded to see how bad Danny's skin looked already. The freezer might have kept pieces of him from falling off prematurely, but his skin already had started going pallid and gray. Just as well, considered D.J., because Lucy had refused to work on him. The most she had been willing to do was swab his palms with some lube while Jack and T.J. held him. That way, if he did grab a hold of Sextasy before she made her "escape into the living room set," she stood a good chance of being able to slip out of his grasp.

As Danny approached a genuinely terrified looking Sextasy, Dave patted himself on the back for having sent T.J. out to snap off the chunk of the Lexus steering wheel. Dave had banged the jagged section of wheel into Danny's chest with a hammer. Danny truly looked like a car crash victim. Tearing out select pieces of T-shirt—most notably the Sextreme Sinema logo—made it look all the more realistic. Dave was certain that anybody who saw this would believe that Danny had been freshly killed in a car accident. It looked flawless.

Danny took a shaky step forward, his bent erection jabbing at Sextasy's crotch as she backed away. She put her hands up, as if to ward the reanimate off and, like he had been cued, he reached up and clamped her wrists in his greasy, cold palms.

The coke wore off the second Emily felt the reanimate's hands on her. She lost the trance-like state she'd struggled to put herself into during the masturbation portion of the scene. Now that she was face to face with the reanimate, now that she could feel his hardness pressing through the dress and against her lips, all bets were off. She was rapidly freaking out.

Sextasy cried out, and it sounded like a whimper. She wrenched her hands free, and backed away from the advancing corpse.

Danny had surprising spring in his step, thought Dave, as he followed the reanimate's progress. He plodded through the kitchen, and was barely a step behind her when she hit the arm of the couch in the living room set.

For a brief second, Sextasy stood toe-to-toe with the reanimate. She lost her breath as he grabbed for her. *Would he actually try to kiss her?* She was unwilling to find out. She threw herself backwards over the arm of the couch, feeling the seams of the red dress tearing loose as she fell.

Exposed now, her legs parted around the reanimate's hips, Sextasy began to madly kick and thrash beneath it. His hands clawed at her breasts, his fingernails scratching her in spots, peeling off his fingertips. And then she felt it—cold, hard pressure spreading her open and invading her. She howled as he sunk his cock into her depths.

His thrusts were jerky and erratic. His bent member was pressing uncomfortably against her dry, inner walls. When he finally seemed as if he were going to complete the act, Sextasy felt his cold tip painfully stab against her cervix. He was losing his balance, toppling over onto her. Sextasy was screaming at the top of her lungs, trying to free herself from beneath the full weight of the reanimate. Her screams were real now, bloodcurdling shrieks of terror, not the phony wails of mock ecstasy. From the corner of her eye, she could see the crew watching, mesmerized. They just stood there, filming. *They have no idea*, she thought, *no idea.*

Couldn't they tell that her screams were real?

Or worse yet, they knew. And they didn't care.

Emily groaned, tried to get her bearings. She put her hands over her ears, hoping that the ringing in them would subside. When it only dimmed, she realized that it wasn't her head that was ringing, but her phone.

Seven-thirty? Who the hell was calling her this early in the morning, especially on Saturday? Probably a motherfucking telemarketer, she fumed.

"Emmie honey? It's Mom, are you there? Well, I just wanted to call you because I haven't heard from you in over a week. I wanted to make sure that everything out there is all right," the gentle, if slightly wavering, voice continued. "And I also wanted to know - *you haven't been spreading your legs for reanimates, have you, you stinking whore?*"

Emily's head shot up and a searing bolt of pain shot through it. She struggled to overcome a wave of nausea and failed, tossing her upper body over the side of the bed and retching violently onto the floor. After a few shaky moments, she got a hold of herself and managed to sit up.

The phone wasn't ringing, it wasn't even on the charger. Of course, her mother hadn't left any messages, either. Even if she was capable of using the phone, it was four-thirty in the morning in Pennsylvania and the odds were small that her mother, even in a rare, lucid moment, could remember Emily's number.

The most recent nightmare sent shivers up her spine, even though the apartment felt abnormally warm. Her stomach was still uneasy, and her tongue felt like somebody had lacquered it and coated it with cotton balls. All in all, she felt like she had just gone a few rounds with Christy Martin, although luckily without any bruising.

What day was it? Emily had no idea. What night had they shot? Wednesday? Thursday? It was all a blur. She knew that Saturday had come, because Lauren had called and beeped and tried the cell phone until she had finally answered.

"Sorry, bad flu," Emily had lied and hung up. If memory served her, she was deep into a bottle of Cuervo Gold while waiting for a little home delivery from Rory, her trustworthy, and very flaming dealer. She thought she remembered seeing him more than once, which undoubtedly meant she had. If she thought she remembered two visits, how many had he made that she didn't remember? Emily decided to wait a minute before moving to the kitchen. As much as she wanted a cold glass of water to wash away the taste of paste in her mouth, she tempered that with actually walking past the open blinds and into the bright sunlight in the kitchen. Any other morning she would have welcomed that warm, cheery spot in her home, but the comfort of the absolute darkness of the bedroom wrapped her like a security blanket.

Emily checked the caller ID box next to her answering machine. Five more calls from Lauren, one from Rory, and one from Vivid. She had a meeting with them on Tuesday, it was probably one of the guys calling to confirm. Emily tapped the *PLAY* button and poised her finger over the *ERASE* key.

"Hi there baby, it's me, I was just cal—" Lauren. "Message deleted. New message, Sunday, 3:47 PM... Hello, Sunshine! It's you-know-who." Rory. He always sounded like he was about to break into a Broadway show tune the way his voice rose and fell when he spoke. "Anyhoo, thanks for thinking of *moi* to cater your little get-together the other night. Just one thing, darling, please, *please* give me a little advance warning. That sort of order ain't won tons and fried rice, you know. Anyway, thanks again, and hey, am I going to be invited to the next little party you're throwing or are you only inviting straight folk? I mean, really hon, a nice, flamboyant man of the new millennium could use some of that cock you're turning away. Well, toodles, sweetie. Call me."... "Em, it's me again. How are you fee— " Lauren again. "Message deleted."... "New message, Monday, 5:53 PM... 'Emmie? You there, it's—' Message deleted."... "New message, Monday, 8:48 PM... 'Em, I'm getting wor—' Message deleted."

Emily was growing exasperated. Cold water, even if it meant braving the kitchen, was starting to sound better and better. "New message, Wednesday, 11:03 AM... 'Sextasy? Lou, just wanted to know what happened yesterday. We waited at Sushi on Sunset until four and tried your cell all afternoon. I really need to hear back from you on *Brigit Ho's Diary*, if not, we're going to go with somebody else, okay? Just let me know. Bye.'... End of messages."

Wednesday? Emily's head, which had just seemed to be settling, spun. Had she lost an entire week? It didn't seem possible, but that was the way it was looking. She searched the clutter by her nightstand for her cell phone. She found it on the floor, next to a crushed plastic tumbler and an empty bottle of Cuervo 1800.

Dead. Not a good sign. She marched over to her computer table. She had left the monitor on, but it had gone dark. She hit the space bar and the screen came to life.

The AOL screen was up. She saw the sign on screen and noted the message: *YOUR ACCOUNT HAS BEEN LOGGED OFF DUE TO INACTIVITY. PLEASE SIGN ON AGAIN LATER.* Emily entered her password, and heard the familiar, "*Welcome! You've got mail.*"

"I'll bet," she thought. The main window appeared. Emily gasped.

Friday. It wasn't Wednesday already, it was Friday. The sour taste in her mouth was returning. Emily tapped the arrow next to the Internet address box. Where had she been when she last logged off? The answer came as the Internet window loaded—The Pennsylvania First National Bank Web site.

Emily logged in to the site. She only wanted to see one element of her account: recent activity. When the info flashed on screen, Emily came dangerously close to throwing up again.

Eight withdrawals, all from cash machines. Rough total, eleven thousand dollars, four of it on Saturday. That explained Rory's cryptic message. She'd catered a party all right, except she hadn't bothered to invite any guests.

Emily dropped her head into her hands and sat there shaking. This was the way it had been the week of the overdose. Her memory nonexistent, her behavior totally out of control. When she had pulled herself together, she checked one last figure before signing off.

She was relieved. The six figure deposit was there, she hadn't imagined it. The eleven grand was repulsive, but only a small dent, nothing that was jeopardizing the overall picture.

Not yet. But it would. If she stayed, she wouldn't be able to escape that. She knew there was no alternative. Delaying was only going to leave her in the same rut, treading water as she stopped accumulating cash and started blowing it. She'd done it before, with tragic consequences. She wasn't going to let that part of her history repeat itself. Her decision was already made—she was getting out and getting out now.

Dave hadn't expected this. In all the scenarios he'd played out in his head, and he had certainly played out some negative ones, this hadn't even seemed a remote possibility. Now, parked in the long term lot at LAX, he took a deep breath and pondered what was next. T.J. was in the passenger seat of the Escalade, his own car stored at his brother-in-law's. He'd been in a rental for the past two days, ever since the Feds had shown up at his apartment complex looking to ask questions about a certain videotape rumored to contain some quite illegal activity. He was lucky that the Feds hadn't got past Phil, the complex manager. Yeah, they had mentioned a videotape they were interested in asking T.J. about, but that wasn't all that unusual.

Phil had one of the nicer complexes in L.A. He'd also gotten a reputation for keeping the activities of his residents quiet. Phil had, at one time or another, rented to half the talent in the industry. He knew how to keep his mouth shut when cops came sniffing around, which was more than an occasional occurrence at the complex. The maintenance there was particularly high for little more than the pool and a swing-up entry gate. However, there was a service not mentioned in the lease that was also included in the fee—if somebody came around looking for you, with or without a warrant, Phil would tip you off. Like he had just done for T.J., by disabling his entry gate card.

When T.J.'s realized his gate card wasn't going to allow him into the complex, he rolled into a nearby 7-11 and dialed the manager's office. Phil picked up on the second ring.

"Hi, Phil, how's it going?" Phil recognized T.J.'s voice immediately.

"Hey, man, not bad, You had two packages come today, they looked like they were pretty expensive. I didn't want to leave them outside, and I couldn't get my master key to open your door, so I put them in my office for a while." T.J. decoded Phil's message. Two guys, well-dressed. Feds, not local cops, not with LAPD's budget. They'd asked Phil to look around, but Phil had the broken key thing to deflect them. They'd had no warrant, but T.J. was betting they had left planning to get one.

"Thanks, I appreciate that."

"Hey, if you want to stop by and pay the rent, I'm gonna be free all morning. I'll fix that problem you were having with the gate, too."

"Yeah, thanks, will do." T.J. hung up and hopped back in the car. Phil got T.J.'s gate card back up and running, knowing that the coast would likely be clear for a few hours, That was enough time for T.J. to cover his ass and get rid of whatever the flatfoots were looking for. Or, to forfeit his security deposit and drop off his key in the rent drop box.

When T.J. stepped into the manager's office minutes later, Phil did not look surprised, but rather, disappointed.

"You didn't bring me a Big Gulp?"

"They were all out of diet, big man."

"But I don't drink diet," came Phil's retort.

"That's why you're the big man," T.J. shot back at the Hawaiian. Rumor had it that back in the seventies, Phil had been talent for a slew of pre-VHS flicks. Now, easily weighing in at three hundred and twenty-five pounds, most new tenants dismissed it. But T.J. believed it. Jette Black was one of Phil's former customers. She claimed he was swinging a ten-inch bat. Iif anybody knew how to eyeball talent, it was Jette, who only gagged when a guy resembled a kielbasa more than a human being.

"Suits?" T.J. asked.

Phil nodded.

"DEA?"

"I don't think so," Phil opined. He was probably right—he'd met up with agents from just about every law enforcement organization over the years. "They were asking about your schedule and if I knew if you had been doing any shooting this week."

"What did you tell 'em?" T.J. asked.

The big Hawaiian laughed. "I told him I sure hoped so. This is porn, I told them. You don't shoot all the time, you can't pay the rent."

"Thanks," responded T.J.

"So, you gonna pay the rent?" asked Phil.

"Yeah, you bet," T.J. confirmed. "Whatever they were nosing around for I'm not worried about it. But I did just have a pretty good run in Vegas the past two days. I'm going down to the sun and sand and easy living under the Federales for a while.

"Sweet. You need any help in breaking in some new, young talent down there?" asked the big Hawaiian. "I been needing a vacation myself, you know."

T.J. shook his head. "Nope, no talent run. Just real, honest-to-goodness R&R, sorry."

When T.J. had first moved into the complex, he hadn't much liked Phil. He had a thing for young girls, and everybody in the place knew it. Once, Phil had T.J. up in the manager's suite. T.J. had been privy to a screening of one of Phil's special import tapes. Teen Asian runaway stuff. Fake, but low-budget enough to look real. The girls might have been legal, but that didn't stop them from dressing like fourteen year olds. Or looking like twelve year olds when their clothes came off. The sex wasn't even all that hot, but that wasn't really what the video was about. It was the fringe element of the fantasy, the kidnap and rape part. T.J. had declined a follow-up invite some months later. Phil had understood. There had been no further invites.

"Hey, you guys aren't shooting any Tracies out there, are you?" Phil asked.

"Tracies" was a reference to Traci Lords, who'd shot a slew of blazing hardcore flicks when she was underage. She was sixteen at the time, though some people thought the first few might have been done when she was actually only fifteen. If you could get good copies, they went for about five hundred dollars. T.J. wondered if Phil was asking because of the visit from the Feds, or for his own reasons.

"Nah, we leave the young girl stuff alone. *Hustler* can take the heat with *Barely Legal*. Less heat we have to deal with, the better."

"Aah, okay. I hear you." T.J. slipped the big Hawaiian an envelope full of fifties. Rent for at least another month, plus a little bonus. He winked at Phil, who didn't even bother to count it. At least not in T.J.'s presence.

T.J. hopped into his car and shot off towards his unit. He didn't want to spend any unnecessary time hanging around, no matter how good Phil's sixth sense was. The faster he booked his flight—to Tahiti and not Mexico as he'd let on to Phil—the better off he was going to be.

He was thinking about Phil as he watched the big Hawaiian come out of the manager's office and head over towards the pool, where he could usually be found. Ostensibly to keep an eye on things. Now that it was summertime, those things were most likely the kids.

T.J. had initially been repulsed by Phil, but the longer he worked in the business, the more he'd come to understand the big Hawaiian.

Phil wasn't a freak because of his fantasies, he'd simply been in the biz too long. Long enough that he'd years ago run out of normal ways to get his rocks off. Happened to everybody, sooner or later.

Unless, of course, you knew when to get out.

Was that what Dave was doing? Getting out? T.J. doubted it, but for the first time in their three years working together, T.J. couldn't read him. For the first time also, Dave didn't look like he had all the answers.

If Dave didn't have all the answers, though, T.J. was certain he had more of the questions—more than he had been willing to let on thus far.

"What about the kid?" Dave asked, breaking the uncomfortable silence.

"Jack took care of it. His dad's got land near Barstow. Jack wrapped him, left him under the floorboards in a little, metal shed. I watched the whole thing. It's one hundred and ten degrees inside if it's ninety outside. He'll be gone by tomorrow."

"Did Jack at least - I mean, he didn't just bur—"

"No, he plugged him first," confirmed T.J. Whatever had spooked Dave had started a conscience growing in him, too. He sure hadn't shown much of one when he'd been using the hammer to pound the blunt end of the steering wheel into Danny's chest.

"Here," said Dave, handing over an envelope. So this was it. Either pay-off money or severance pay. T.J. opened it. There was a thick stack of hundreds inside. "I have to let this thing blow over for a while," Dave explained. "Marcus doesn't even want to touch it." Marcus meant Marcus Minervini, the Sextreme lawyer and brain trust who defended some of the most high-profile names in the industry on any number of charges, ranging from drugs to federal obscenity charges. He was the best of the best, had ties to the mob, and here Dave was telling him that Marcus didn't want to fight. It sounded like Marcus didn't even want to get into the ring.

"How long you think you're leaving for?" T.J. asked.

"I'm thinking a month, maybe two. Dieter wants to see the thing first hand. He understands the heat, but he has a shadow company over there he can use to start recouping some of the cash. Ivan doesn't care what we do, he's secure based on *Cum Freaks*. He knows he's getting paid back no matter what."

"Dieter isn't worried?"

"No, he has concerns. But he's got a few countries over there where he could distribute it. Places where there aren't necrophilia laws on the books. Yet."

"So much for a big US release," sighed T.J., who wondered if there was any way the Feds could prove who had been present at the studio that night.

"Dieter thinks we should stream it on a password protected site out of the Ukraine for $39.95. He's looking into getting the servers set up."

"Good idea."

"What about the studio, everything there taken care of?"

"Yeah. We repainted the flats, got rid of all the props. Donated the furniture to four different charities. The cleaning crew did a white tornado on the place, and we painted the whole floor over. The rent is paid through the end of the lease. The computer is in pieces, we tossed it out on the way to Barstow. We're clean. The two dykes we paid to fluff Danny up both have records, so they won't say shit. We shredded their releases and IDs anyway. My guess is that in six months they'll be out of the biz entirely, be crack whores, or dead. They were strictly street skanks."

"Okay then. I guess that does it." Dave handed T.J. the keys to the Escalade. "You'll do a magic job and make this disappear pronto, right?"

T.J. nodded. "Yeah, I know a chop shop I can take it to. By ten tonight it'll be in pieces and on its way to wherever. You'll be able to make a stolen car report when you get back." T.J. pocketed the keys and reached out to shake Dave's hand. "Have a good trip. Stay in touch."

"I'll call you from Germany," Dave said, grabbing his carry-on from the back seat. T.J. doubted it.

Sextreme, he was sure, had just gone out of business.

Emily went downstairs to the hospital pay phone and looked around. She didn't know why, considering that there was no reason for anybody to be suspicious of her. She hardly looked like America's number one sex goddess now, dressed in an oversized fleece jogging suit that nearly concealed the fact that she had any breasts at all. She had no make-up on and her hair was cut short. A home dye job had turned platinum blonde tresses back to dirty blonde. The lips were still there, there was nothing she could do about them except wait out the collagen. The lack of sleep since she'd arrived in Pennsylvania had left circles under her eyes, too. She was certain that nobody back home was suddenly going to turn around in the Piggly Wiggly and recognize her as Sextasy Chase. As far as Emily Chassen was concerned, Sextasy Chase was missing and, for all intents and purposes, presumed dead. Hopefully, in time, nobody would bother to even look for her.

Standing at the pay phone, Emily wished she'd waited and used the one at the public library again. The hospital only had a pair of open phones standing back to back. The library still had an actual booth, with a door and a little corner-cut wooden seat. Emily was amazed that there was a touch-tone phone inside—the rest of the booth probably dated back to the year the library had been built, which was sometime in the fifties.

She dialed the 818 area code and waited to hear her—no, Sextasy's—voice come back to her. Soon, Emily's Pennsylvania accent would return and the last traces of Sextasy would disappear from her mannerisms. The implants, she would have to live with.

The split second she heard Sextasy she punched the asterisk on the phone and then her message retrieval code. The machine announced that she had nine messages. She thought it likely that at least eight of them had been left by Lauren. She poised her index finger over the seven on the phone's touch pad—the message delete command. Each time a message began with Lauren's voice, she pushed it without listening further. She had been nearly prophetic. Seven from Lauren, each growing more and more angry at her for ignoring her calls. The last two messages were both from Dave. The first was brief and to the point.

"Hi, hon. Listen, I have to go out of town for a while. If you need to get in touch with me, leave a message on the service, I'll call you back. Bye."

Emily thought Dave sounded a little bit rushed. The second message, left eight hours ago, explained why.

"Hey, babe. Listen, we got some problems popping up on this end. I think if you were planning that trip we talked about, now's the time to book it. We're running into a few legal details on that last project, so I'm going overseas to try and do some negotiating. I'll let you know when I'm back in town. Take care of yourself."

Emily replayed the message once, purged it, and hung up. Legal problems meant bad news. If Dave was going overseas, it meant he was hiding. Dave hated to fly and was terrified of flying over an ocean. If he was going to that length, it wasn't to negotiate, it was to disappear. What that meant for the tape, she didn't know. She could only hope against hope that it meant it would never see the light of day, although that was doubtful. If Pam and Tommy couldn't keep their home movies secret, this footage had no chance of simply disappearing.

Emily felt more drained by the phone call than she had spending the night at the hospital. She longed to go back home and get a decent night's sleep, but guilt denied her. Instead, she washed her face in the ladies' room and trudged back upstairs. Maybe today her mother would stir.

A nurse was standing over her mother's bed when Emily entered the room. From the size of her ass, it was Colleen, likely doing the afternoon rounds.

"Anything?" Emily asked. The nurse turned a pudgy cheek towards her.

"No, nothing. I'm sorry. You know, you should really go home and get some rest. If there's any change, we'll certainly call you."

"Maybe you're right," Emily promised. "I have to change into some fresh clothes, anyway." She could tell that fat Colleen didn't believe her, but she didn't blame her. Emily had been saying the same thing for the past two days. The sweatsuit was getting gamey, though. Today, she really would have to head home.

Fat Colleen left the room. Emily dropped back down in the chair where she spent most of the last few days and nights. On the nightstand beside her mother, in the shadow of all the machinery that blocked the window, was the stack of books she had pulled out of the library. *The Horse Whisperer*, *Black Beauty*, *National Velvet*. She was almost done with them. She would have to ask the librarian for help when she returned them. They were the only books about horses—her mother's favorite thing in the world—she knew of. Emily had been reading aloud to her mother since she'd arrived. It did little to assuage her guilt, but it was the only thing she could think of doing. It was something.

"I gotta run up to the house for a little bit, Mom. I'll finish reading to you when I come back this afternoon." She stroked her mother's tiny, wrinkled hand. The veins showed through her skin like it was paper. She had gotten so small and weak that it almost hurt to look at her. She wouldn't show that, though. Not here, even if her mother wasn't aware of her presence. She kissed her mother on the cheek, careful not to touch the oxygen mask, then turned, and rushed out of the room before the tears came.

Driving home, Emily collected herself and tried to think about happier times. That was difficult, however, because that always came around to Emily's leaving, which she knew had broken her mother's heart. Emily reflected on it. Her mother had never gotten over her father leaving, and then her one joy, her own daughter, followed suit. No wonder the woman had gotten so sick.

Stop it, Emily told herself. The Alzheimer's hadn't been her fault. She had no control over that.

But what about the stroke? What about the stress when the tax people had started calling her because Emily hadn't sent the money to them? She had put her mother off for the better part of a year, telling the frail, old woman that it was all a mistake. What else could she do? Admit that she had forged power of attorney papers to take over her finances and spent the tax money on herself? Admit to her mother that she had put the woman in the hole for over a hundred thousand dollars, most of which Emily had put up her nose? The Alzheimer's had struck at a coincidentally opportune time. But even when her mother had been shifted into the nursing home, Emily wondered—had her mother suspected? Had she figured things out before the disease had provided Emily with the perfect cover?

Emily shook her head violently, trying to shake the potential truth out of mind. She was making it all right now, after all. The government had gotten close, but they hadn't foreclosed, and now they had been paid in full, thanks to a cashier's check and the current year's property taxes in advance. She could still forge her mother's name—all that practice on report cards that had never made it home—and now, she had the deed and title in her name, free and clear. She was finally back home, except home was empty. She was too late and the thought tore her apart. She tossed back a Pepto-Bismol tablet to combat the nausea. If she was lucky, her mother would at least open her eyes one more time, so they could see each other. That was important, that she at least open her eyes and see her daughter one more time. Emily was sure that her mother would know. Even with the Alzheimer's and the stroke, she would know. Her daughter had kept her promise—she'd come home.

At the house, the second step on the front porch creaked, just as it had when she was a teen. The rope swing where she'd played every afternoon after school, and where Jimmy Petersen had given her her first kiss, was still there. Emily was going to have new ropes hung to replace the rotting ones her father had installed so many years before. Back when she had begged him for a swing. She had been eight then. They had still been a family.

The ancient, wrought iron mailbox was stuffed. Much the same it had been every day in the weeks since she'd returned. Her mother had somehow managed to get herself on every imaginable mailing list in the country. Lonely, maybe? Looking to fill the box because promised letters never seemed to arrive?

A large, padded envelope caught her eye. It was addressed to no recipient, only to the address. It had a Packages Plus return address label. Emily slipped it free from the junk mail, which she piled with the rest on the kitchen table. The Packages Plus envelope was from California. Mail forwarded from her private mail box.

The envelope didn't contain much. Two collection notices from the BMG Music Club, demanding payment for CDs she didn't plan on paying for. They were addressed to Melony Citase, as was a bill from Packages Plus, requiring payment if she wanted to continue her service. Emily had intentionally let the "H" on her application appear to be two letters. The Pakistani working the counter hadn't paid any attention, hadn't even asked her for ID when she'd opened the account. Ah, L.A., where low expectations never failed to be met. There was a phone bill, which she discarded—she didn't care about Melony's credit report—and a copy of *Adult Video News*. The cover caught her eye.

Emily found herself staring at a ghost. There on the cover was Sextasy staring back at her. But it was not a glamour shot. The photo was not retouched and not retouched on purpose. Whoever ran it wanted her skin to look flat and lifeless. Her eye color was drained and her pupils were reduced to black saucers. There were also marks on her arms that were eerily familiar—she recognized them from the Discovery Channel. She stiffened when she read the coverline.

"Corpse Cover-Up?" leapt out at her in fifty point type. Beneath, even worse. "Did Sextasy Chase Put the Feel-Ya in Necrophilia?"

Emily tore into the magazine. It appeared every article, every department dealt with the tape. Some people claimed to have been there when it was shot. Others said that they had a copy. The legal forum was covering it, too. Apparently, necrophilia was a prosecutable offense. And, unnamed sources had let a columnist at *AVN* know that the FBI was interested in the male talent featured on the video. They had a lot of questions for anybody they could find who might have information on the tape.

The tape. It wasn't the *alleged tape*. Of course it wasn't. In the main feature, there was a video capture. Emily was in the red dress, pulling out her tit. But there in the background you could make out the eyes of somebody looking in on her. Someone with the top of their head caved in.

Emily shut the magazine and threw it on the table. She knew that she hadn't heard the last of the tape, but she hadn't imagined that doing the tape had made her a criminal. Her eyes drifted back to the cover, she couldn't help it. She took a long, hard look.

Staring into the face of death was nothing new. She had been doing so, in a way, every day in the weeks since she had been home. Her mother's face, after all, was hers. Everybody always remarked as she had grown that she had always looked like her mother. She didn't share a single, noticeable trait of her father. Seeing the grip of death on herself in youth wasn't nearly as unsettling as it was in the face of her own flesh and blood. Pictures paled in comparison to the real thing, she realized. Then something else caught her eye. It was almost insignificant, tucked in a tuft of her platinum blonde tresses, just under the masthead.

September. AVN had had to rush this issue's content into print fast. They had only shot the tape nine weeks earlier. Nine weeks in publishing was hardly enough.

Nine weeks. Emily felt her stomach lurch as she ran towards the bathroom. Bile welled up in her throat and she threw her face in the toilet as the heaves came uncontrollably. Nine weeks, she thought. It had been nine weeks since she had that rotted, reanimate cock inside her. Now, the realization struck her like the bouts of nausea she had been experiencing every morning.

She was late.

ACKNOWLEDGEMENTS

If you ever find yourself questioning how many friends you have, write a book. When you get to the people you want to thank, and don't want to leave out, see how many times you add to it so that you don't forget anybody.

As for me, I gotta start with Ed Shulusky, who wore out a few lead pipes beating some of the first drafts into shape for this book. Usually, getting a good edit on something means getting a second set of eyes on it. In this case, it meant a first set. In addition to Ed, there's Liz, who also did a great job with her draft, and who was not *too* unkind with the red pen. Don't worry, Liz, I'll replace that case of Bics you went through. And there's Judy, the farm girl, who worked with the printer on the production of this book.

As for the group of people who had less direct influence, but have helped me in one way or another, here are my "liner notes." For starters, the two people who did have a direct influence, of course, my parents, who, while not always enjoying my choice of genres, were nevertheless 110% supportive every step of the way. Marjorie Harris, who recognized the difference between incompetence and creativity when I got bounced out of advanced English by a stodgy, ancient teacher who didn't believe the semicolon had any place in high school English papers. Marge Harris taught me more about writing and following my instincts than any professor I encountered in high school or college. Kevin Clement, who runs the best convention on the East Coast, the Chiller Theatre Expo. His support and friendship over the years is one of the reasons that missing a few of those shows the past two years were truly dark moments. Fred Greenberg, whose support since the very beginning of my comic book career was unflagging, and whose personal friendship became even more valuable to me over the years. To the other Fred, and my gang of buddies up in Valley Stream, many of which got to read a lot of the crap I wrote ever before the possibility of a book was in the offing. Andrea, Michael that Dog, and the people who make the Crime and Criminals group the place to be if you're into true crime. With luck, I'll be joining them again soon. My friends at Crescent in New York, who I miss working with dearly, and who I gave a few cameos in this work. To my buddies at The SCORE Group, particularly John and Sue, who gave me incredible latitude and the ability to do a job far longer than I could have imagined any other owners doing. Also, to Elliot James, who is a font of information and keeps me in the game, and Robert Morales, the reason I have so many 2nd place softball trophies on my shelves. Dr. J. Harris Levy, who had a lousy patient for a year and a half, but kept my eyes open long enough to get ready for what was next. Now that I think about it, he's a huge basketball fan, and I never called him Dr. J. How'd I miss that? When I run my first charity event, I'll hold this over his head to guarantee that he shows up.

I would be remiss to ignore my friend Al, my wheels and partner in crime on weekly prowls out to the Goth clubs where being totally in the dark doesn't matter all that much, and where I recharge the mental batteries as often as I can. And finally, Pam, without whom this book would not be finished at all. Without whom I probably wouldn't be as far along as I am in such a short period of time. Without whom I think things would be quite a bit worse. She doesn't always know it, but it's true. There is nobody with whom I would rather navigate what comes next, than her.

On a special note...

There are two people who would be on this page whether or not they had any involvement with this book. The first, is Bernie Wrightson. Had Bernie said no to doing the illos for this project, he'd still be reading this. I got to meet Bernie at the very first comic show I ever did, and by sheer luck smiling down upon me, we eventually became friends. More valuable to me than the images he's provided on these pages, I think about a night in March of last year sitting in my kitchen, after I'd been forced to bail out of an appearance we were to have done together in Orlando. We stayed up all night, talking about the creative process, herpetology, old movies, getting older, where we had lived...everything but comic books and work. It's the kind of conversation you have with people who are really friends, and not just people you work with. In my life, I have been fortunate enough to have enjoyed years worth of Bernie's artwork. Now that that's no longer possible, it's much easier to recognize that I'm much more fortunate to enjoy his friendship.

And finally, there's Hart, as much my brother as if we shared a bloodline. He did all the production work on the covers, made my first hardcover and paperback look pretty. All that aside, he is the best friend that I could ever have hoped to have. He's the only person I'd work with without any more than a nod and a handshake. He is the person who I've gone to the wall with before, and would gladly put my back against the brick alongside again, any time, any place. He offered me the opportunity to write the introduction to his book, and I felt honored to do so. Recently, Pam threw me a surprise birthday party, which happened to occur during a particularly brutal stretch for me. Friends and relatives were there, and it was a helluva surprise. Then, out of the blue (or black, in my case), who steps out but Hart. The party was my present, but his being there was the part I'll never forget. That was the highlight, the best part of a largely forgettable birthday. As with Bernie, Hart's a talented individual whose efforts it's been a pleasure to have been exposed to. But, it's his friendship which I cannot accurately describe that I appreciate most of all. I think they both know this, but it's nice to have a place to write it down.

—JM
November 2002

Every day you haven't written,
is a day you've written off.